Dancing in the Desert

May you find joy
in the midst of your
deserts -

Beverly

Published by The Ark Family Preservation Center, an imprint of Cool River Pub, Inc.
https://thearkfamily.org/

ISBN: 978-1-7325420-4-4
ISBN: 978-1-7325420-5-1 (e-book)

Cover and interior design: Bill Kersey, KerseyGraphics

Printed in the United States of America

Living Boldly in Dry Places

Dancing in the Desert

a memoir

Beverly J. Oxley

THE Ark
FAMILY PRESERVATION CENTER

Endorsements

As I read *Dancing in the Desert,* Dr. Beverly Oxley's memoir, I felt guided by a strange and beautiful sense of hope. She welcomes readers to dance during their own dry seasons. We can relate. Pain visits us. Questions come. Tsunamis interrupt our plans. How are we affected? How do we endure? How do we get better? Dr. Oxley's narrative helps readers address those questions and deal with hurts in a way that heals the spirit. Welcome to the desert. Begin to dance. And be better from it.

Chris Maxwell
Author, Pastor, Spiritual Director

This is an amazing and inspiring story! It is also an important book. Dr. Oxley's willingness to open the shaded windows of her life will surprise and encourage many. Her analysis of the brokenness in American families is distressing because it is so destructive and so widespread. Thank God that she and others stand in the gap for these families. That story will grip readers. Perhaps that compelling and emotional narrative will also take many to new depths of prayer and action for those battered by the harsh realities of modern life.

Dr. A. D. Beacham, Jr.
General Superintendent, International
Pentecostal Holiness Church

As a foster/adoptive mom, *Dancing in the Desert* captivated me from the moment I began reading. I know how real these issues are. I have stood in the wreckage of "the demonic, putrid, and heartbreaking details of sexual abuse, domestic violence, and addictions." I thank God for the faith and obedience of Dr. Oxley in this journey.

The Christian world I grew up in often overlooked the Lord's words in this matter, "religion that God our Father accepts as pure and faultless is this: to look after orphans and widows in their distress and to keep oneself from being polluted by the world." Beverly Oxley drove directly into the heart of the storm.

Shanna Kohr
Mom, student

Dedication

To Marigny and Parisa, my granddaughters
You did not know your requests for bedtime stories from my childhood would lead to a book. Neither did I. When you read this a few years from now, you will learn the rest of those stories.

Marigny Julip and Parisa Mazarine Whalen, granddaughters

Guiding Scriptures and Quotes

"You turned my wailing into dancing; you removed my sackcloth and clothed me with joy;"

– Psalm 30:11

"Where can I go from your Spirit? Where can I flee from your presence? If I go up to the heavens, you are there; if I make my bed in the depths, you are there. If I rise on the wings of the dawn, if I settle on the far side of the sea, even there your hand will guide me, your right hand will hold me fast.

– Psalm 139:7-10

Whatever you do, work at it with all your heart, as working for the Lord, not for human masters.

– Colossians 3:23

Religion that God our Father accepts as pure and faultless is this: to look after orphans and widows in their distress and to keep oneself from being polluted by the world.

– James 1:27

"...what does the Lord your God ask of you but to fear the Lord your God, to walk in obedience to him, to love him, to serve the Lord your God with all your heart and with all your soul?"

– Deuteronomy 10:12

The only thing necessary for the triumph of evil is for good men to do nothing.

– Edmund Burke, 1770

It is not how much we are doing but how much love, how much honesty, how much faith is put into doing it.

– Mother Teresa, "Her People and Her Work"

Cheered by the presence of God, I will do at each moment, without anxiety, according to the strength which He shall give me, the work that His Providence assigns me. I will leave the rest without concern; it is not my affair.

– François de Salignac de la Mothe-Fénelon

Table of Contents

Foreword

Recommending the reading of a memoir is an uneasy task for me, a retired college professor in philosophy, theology, and Biblical studies. Since this memoir comes from my wife of 51 years, conventional wisdom warns me, "I know too much. What about her flaws not talked about in the book?" Add to this, recent research in brain science which raises doubts about the reliability of human remembrance, casting possible suspicion of fallibility upon Beverly's record of life-memories. And even Beverly's use of editorial readers could leave me unsettled: "Did this event really happen like this?" Nevertheless, it is my awareness of the three potential issues — flaws, fallibility and fiction — that motivates me to say that this is a 'must-read' book based upon what I know.

For one thing, I know that this memoir should be read because its quality of writing reflects editorial excellence in its trustworthy stories. Excellence is Beverly's gift to you, the reader; excellence is a feature of what Beverly pursues because the desire for excellence is who she is. Thus, a variety of editorial readers, friends - even myself – have read various versions and offered suggestions for improvement. You, the reader, can be assured that every word in this memoir has been chosen, sometimes in the agony of birthing a special nuance, by Beverly herself.

Excellence for Beverly has meant keeping her life-story from getting bogged down in tedium. To achieve this, she did many rewrites and tried out many book-titles.

Excellence also means Beverly's writing style varies. Some of her paragraphs are like a documentary; some are insights of a PhD educator; some flare with color and humor. After all, how could it be Beverly's memoir without her trade-mark laughter – unexpected, natural, a surprising agent of healing. Whatever the literary form, Beverly wants her writings to have an excellence in pointing to God, quietly and openly.

Second, I know that the memoir's historical veracity has been tested by readers who knew Beverly in her various lifespans covered in the book. If a reader had a differing perspective on the way an event might have happened, the event was researched or omitted in the memoir. I firmly believe the events discussed in this memoir are trustworthy. I have always been – and continue to be – amazed at Beverly's memory, especially her ability to remember birthdates of family and friends. (In pre-cell phone days her memory contained a contact list of telephone numbers!)

Third, and most importantly, what I know about the author as a person, my wife, pushes urging the reading of her memoir. World literature, from epic poetry to children's legends to popular self-help books, is filled with stories of those overcoming disadvantaged childhoods through survival opportunities, extraordinary will, and hard work. But I know that there is a difference in Beverly's memoir. I have read her "living memoir" (2 Corinthians 3:3) and this much I know: God has been at work in her story 'behind the scenes.' As she recalls events in her life, ordinary stories take on an extraordinary significance. She looks back and sees how God has graciously brought good out of some of her life's most difficult moments.

Beverly's life has been abundantly blessed of God. In diverse and surprising ways God has been at work guiding her journey when she, herself, was unaware of where the future would lead her. In her memoir, she looks back at how God brought people into her life who became role-models and God's messengers to her – such as an elementary school teacher, a devoted aunt, a blind musician – even when they may have been unaware of their being used by God.

God has used her studies of Biblical characters, from Moses to Jesus, to help her define her purpose in life. From her childhood days of feeling overlooked to her first teaching job, to her providing therapy to hurting children, to her establishing a counseling center and being its CEO, to her founding a non-profit to preserve families, and to her filling up her role as a grandmother, to feeling responsible to care for an aging husband, Beverly sees her whole life through the lens of duty to help others.

As you will discover in her book, Beverly is preeminently a heart-person, a psychologist who knows feelings can often be more important than facts in shaping the way a person sees things. Yet, I believe that her ability to remember so clearly her childhood or adolescent feelings contribute to why she is such an effective therapist. She understands the abused child, the frustrated teenager, and those who have suffered painful losses.

Without doubt, I know that God has used special experiences to speak to her. In one life-transforming occasion described in Chapter 8, when God showed her the hardness of her heart toward her father, she responded so dramatically in accepting God's genuine forgiveness, she "...danced audaciously in the desert," as only someone can who has been released from years of bondage.

While Beverly continues to face the expected aging challenges, I am confident the God who transforms desert places into springs of living water will continue to guide, sustain, and enable her remarkable journey to flourish. As you read her story, I pray you will also discover this just and merciful God of surprises is at work in your own life.

In closing this Foreword, I want to give personal praise, not merely for the book, but for its author, the 'wife of my youth,' Dr. Beverly J. Oxley. As the Biblical book of Proverbs 12:4 teaches, she is a "...wife of noble character who is her husband's crown." The Hebrew word in Proverbs for "noble character" means to be courageous (Proverbs 12:4, 31:10, 31:29). It takes courage to speak up against a wayward father; it takes courage to speak up for truth in a court of law deciding the destiny of a foster child; it takes courage to repent; it takes courage to forgive; it takes courage as a woman in a male-dominated society to initiate something new - a counseling center or non-profit benefiting children and families.

To be sure, the Proverbs 31 description is not a template for all wives. But when one finds such a wife whom God calls to serve and empowers with "noble character" to "live boldly in dry places," she is to be honored. While Beverly has honored me by requesting this Foreword, she is to be honored much more. She is, indeed, my "crown."

Paul J. Oxley
Franklin Springs, Georgia
October, 2020

Introduction

Blowing in the Wind

When I was born in Tulare, California, June 8, 1948, the United States had just passed through three historic disruptions—the Great Depression, the Dust Bowl, and World War II—in less than 20 years. Like the blades of a big three-bottom plow, those catastrophic events turned the soil of the whole nation. Then, when the sod had been ripped out, erosion began. The winds blew millions of people away from jobs, communities, safety, health, stability, and hope.

As I am writing this memoir, another historic disruption has arrived: a novel coronavirus, SARS-CoV-2, has created a pandemic (Covid-19) around the world. No one can predict how long, how many deaths, or how much economic damage we will suffer. As with a Category-5 hurricane, after the wind and water abate, land and lives will be forever changed.

Looking back over my life, I have also seen that catastrophic disruptions can bring opportunities for a course correction; vital changes if we are to become better, kinder, more just and generous. We can choose love or hate, justice or selfishness, light or darkness, blessings or curses, life or death (Deuteronomy 30:19). We can tremble in fear behind locked doors. Or we *can* dance boldly on the desert floor.

In my early years, the disruptive national winds blew my family back and forth between California and Oklahoma like tumbleweeds. We lived in two states, six cities, and 13 homes in 12 years. Dad was on the move, chasing his dreams while we just tried to keep up. Mom had four babies in five years. We followed him for 12 years of my life, 13 of my brother Ken's years, and 17 years of Mom's life. Then, suddenly, the winds stopped. No more sudden moves. No more packing up in the middle of the night. That story comes later.

As an adolescent, Homer's epic poem, *The Odyssey*, dropped like a seed into my heart. It helped me to understand something that happened to me at age 9. As Ulysses traveled through islands in the Mediterranean, he knew Sirens, women who sang so beautifully that men jumped ship and never returned home, inhabited one island. That island held the bones of the sailors who could not resist; the wreckage of their ships cluttered the coastline.

Because Ulysses was determined to avoid that fate, he placed wax in his men's ears and told them to tie him to the mast of the ship until they got past the island and could no longer hear the Sirens' music. Sure enough, when Ulysses heard the Sirens' song, he fought to break free to join the beautiful women. But the ropes held him tight.

That seed sprouted when I realized that being tied to the mast of the ship could also keep me from a deadly fate. If I could be held tightly in the arms of the One I trusted, I would remain safe. So, when I was 9, I ceded authority of my life and tied myself to the mast of Jesus Christ. I freely decided to obey whatever He said and accepted His guidance wherever He led, whether or not I understood it.

I did not know at age 9 just how windy life would become. In fact, I don't think I realized the full scope of the Harris and Clinkenbeard families' saga until I wrote this book, looking back at the meandering trail that led to this scenic overlook. I began to see that God Himself made the crooked trail, not me.[1]

Just as Yahweh did not lead the ancient Israelites in a straight line in their Exodus from Egypt to the Promised Land, I could not have walked a straight path either. Just as the Israelites needed to be tested and matured in their faith, His purpose for my zigzagging journey purified and empowered me. God's purpose often requires more circuitous or serrated trails.

Although I intended to always listen to God's voice and follow Him wherever He led, there were times I refused to follow. He didn't cast me away, but faithfully held me to the mast. You will find the details in the pages to come. For now, I will tell you it took seven decades for me to connect the dots of my life. Only then could I glimpse His purpose for my windy and winding journey.

Because I am a private person, writing this book has been tough. That is primarily because I have not shared many of these experiences. Even my daughters have known little about my childhood.

Several friends encouraged me to write my memoirs. I shirked their suggestions for a long time because I felt I had little to share. But then God started tugging my heart about writing my story. What if He could use my life story to encourage others to carry on?

God sees possibilities in you, dreams greater than you can imagine. Yes, you, the reluctant one. You, the impulsive one. You, who runs away from problems or wants to quit. You who desires invisibility. You, who made a mess of your life. You, who even doubts God's existence, much less His Presence within you. *Pay attention!* God may be speaking to you.

1 "Accept the way God does things, for who can straighten what he has made crooked?" – Ecclesiastes 7:13 (NLT)

Think about your family. They need you to be a steadfast courier of generosity and unconditional love. They especially need that in a day of "ME first," arrogance, and cynicism. Your descendants need a dependable, humble person who will say "yes" to the greater good despite the sacrifices required.

Think about your generation. Deceived by cultural slave masters, many now live in bondage. We all know captives to addictions, fears, and cycles of futility. Think of those who just want to be loved and accepted. Think of wanderers who lost their way in the desert; they need a place of rest, refreshment, and renewal. They need someone to get in the trenches with them, to walk with them, encourage them, and guide them to the Promised Land.

You can't do it alone. Nobody can. But, as you will read in these pages, I have learned God is reliable; He will not fade or become bored or get tired. Even when we face cancer, car wrecks, Alzheimer's Disease, moral collapse, divorce, mental breakdowns, lies, and unfaithfulness, God will be there, holding us close and guiding us to our destination. He is fully trustworthy.

Now, I invite you to step into my story. If you read my journey with an open heart, I believe you too will discover what I learned about the God Who created you, the One Who presided over all your days, the One Who inscribed His love and His purpose on your heart. I believe you will discover the amazing, kind, and good God has a significant purpose for you. He desires your constant companionship through all of your life – from the agonies to the ecstasies, from the mundane to the momentous.

Come to think of it, this could be an important book for you to read.

Chapter 1

Born Old

My brother Ken always said I was born old.

And I believed him because he was a year older and knew much more than I did about those things. He says he can remember my talking to adults when I was a little kid. They would talk to me about their problems and I would listen to them. I guess empathy was as natural to me as eating my favorite childhood snack—ten black pitted olives—one for each finger. Much later in life I learned that a precocious self-reliance is common in kids who believe their parents to be unreliable or preoccupied.

My earliest memory was the trauma of an emergency room. At 3, I was screaming my head off. Blood was everywhere. I had busted my chin on the bathtub. I wasn't screaming because of the blood; I was screaming at the needle coming toward my face. The blood-soaked towel wrapped around me didn't help to calm me either.

The doctor called one nurse and then another and then another. It took four nurses to hold me down. Funny how a 3-year-old can acquire super-human strength when she believes more pain is coming. After the shot calmed me down, the doctor sewed up my chin. I wanted to get out of that sterile white hospital. It smelled funny and I wanted back in my parents' safe arms.

Of course, I did not know that the pain of a busted chin is minor league compared to a busted heart. The loneliness following the deaths of close friends and family members, the separation of intimate relationships, and the agony of rejection all surpass physical pain. But, at some point, if we are going to have a life, we have no choice but to make peace with our pain. And I did, but it came 46 years after my busted chin. At some distant point, my emotional pain and I would reconcile.

Bobby

A year later, I spent time at another hospital when we lived in Sacramento. Only that time, I was on the outside of the hospital. Ken and I looked up from the window of our car as our older brother Bobby came to the second-story window of the brick hospital. He waved at us even though he was so weak that dad had to hold him up to the window. I remember his pale face and raccoon-like darkened eyes.

Going to the hospital to see Bobby is my first vivid memory of him; I was barely 4 years old. Bobby knew he was dying and so did everyone else. It wouldn't be long. In a desperate attempt to save Bobby's life, Mom and Dad drove him up the California coastline to Portland, Oregon, where the evangelist Oral Roberts was holding a crusade. Maybe, just maybe, when the preacher prayed for the sick, his prayers would save my 8-year-old brother from death by leukemia.

Mom and Dad had grown up with Oral Roberts in Oklahoma, back before the second world war scattered so many Okies to other parts of the globe. My parents had faith in God, and they also had faith in Oral Roberts. But, as a 4-year-old kid, I had a horrible feeling that Bobby was dying. Even his teeth had grown dark. Mom said it was because of his medicine.

Ken and I had stayed in the car below his window because kids could not enter the hospital. So, there we were, a 4- and 5-year-old languishing in a hot car on a summer day, wishing our brother would come out to play with us, just as he always did. But he didn't. Dad held him in the open window so we could wave at him. Soon, Mom came down to the car with ice cream cones that Bobby wanted to share with us. We knew he loved us.

A few weeks later, Dad held me in his arms so I could say good-bye to my brother lying in the long wooden box. How I loved him! Why did they put Bobby in a box? Why did he look like he was asleep when Dad said he was dead? Was he really sleeping, but pretending to be dead? Even a 4-year-old has questions about death.

They dressed Bobby in the cowboy shirt he loved so much. When a salesman passed through our neighborhood taking pictures of kids on his Shetland pony for a small fee, Bobby sat on the horse outfitted in his cowboy shirt and hat. In that photograph, he sure looked like a real cowboy to me. Even had a red bandana around his neck. I loved that picture of Bobby, and I thought about him on that pony as I looked at him, dressed in his cowboy shirt. He was so still.

Bobby on Shetland pony

I also thought about the day he came home all bloody. Some bullies from school had beaten him up. The buttons on his shirt were torn off and his arm was bleeding. Bobby told us, "They grabbed my arm and slung me around and around and threw me in a ditch." Had I been there, I could have told them he was really, really sick, and that's why he couldn't fight back. I knew Bobby was really an angel; he was so good and kind that he would never hurt anyone. Even if he weren't sick, he wouldn't hurt them. He was my hero, and that was more important than being a good fighter.

I didn't like him being in that box one bit. That was my brother who was kindhearted and gentle with me. That kind of brother should grow up to protect his little sister when she needs him. He should not leave his little brother and sister alone in the world. We needed him. The world needed that kind of boy.

Looking back, I was learning that life was unpredictable, that we can't just wish for things and they come true, and that people we love can vanish in a moment. I learned that life could be painful.

Christopher Columbus Harris

My dad was born in 1926 in Stratford, Oklahoma. He left home when he was 16 – driven from home by his father's harsh temper and leather strap. By that age, he no longer had to put up with that kind of abuse. Dad had a slew of half-siblings from a "his-kids-her-kids" union which then produced four sons who were "our kids." Dad was the oldest of the final four children in the Harris family. His parents named him Christopher Columbus Harris, after his grandfather. He was tall, dark, and handsome. His winsome personality disarmed everyone, at least, in public. At home, maybe not so much. As far as I can remember, he wasn't afraid of anything.

Dad dropped out of school in the third grade to help support his family. Many boys did. The Great Depression sent even prosperous families to the poorhouse. Many people committed suicide because of the shame of poverty. But Dad had acquired a strong work ethic. He and his siblings picked cotton, grew corn, and did odd jobs to put beans and cornbread on the table. He was never without work for more than a few days. And he never spoke of the hardships of his childhood.

Obviously, the poverty of that era left scars on him and most other common folks who had no education or wealth.

But, Dad had somehow caught a glimpse of the American Dream, and he reached for financial success. He lived up to the name

Christopher Columbus Harris (Dad) and Flora Belle Clinkenbeard (Mom) and Bobby

"Christopher Columbus" as a daring adventurer. While chasing his dreams, Dad was like an entrepreneur in search of a new world, a world of material success. That obsession kept his family moving from place to place, job to job, and house to house.

Flora Belle Clinkenbeard

If Dad had an erratic childhood with no educational opportunities, Mom's early years were quite the opposite. The Clinkenbeard family, an intelligent, industrious, and God-honoring family, was the epitome of stability. They valued dutiful, honest, hard work. If Dad lived in a world of romance, with impractical and extravagant notions, Mom lived in a world of realism, with down-to-earth, live-within-your-means desires. No get rich schemes for mom's family. They believed in working hard for every penny earned.

My maternal great-grandparents, James William and Josephine Marsh, part of the Oklahoma Land Run of 1889, homesteaded 160 acres near Prague. That land remains in the family today. My maternal grandmother, Gladys Marsh Clinkenbeard, was born in 1899. When she married Fletcher Clinkenbeard, they moved to Stratford, Oklahoma, 65 miles away.

Flora Belle Clinkenbeard, my mother, was the third of Gladys and Fletcher Clinkenbeard's seven children. She was gentle, soft-spoken, and intelligent. She graduated from Stratford High School at a time when most girls dropped out of school. Her youngest brother, Jack, went on to get a degree in forestry from Oklahoma A & M (now Oklahoma State University). Although Mom's other siblings didn't have college degrees, they all had steady income and a strong faith in God.

Mom's life-pattern was different from her siblings; her marriage was difficult and her family income was unpredictable. But her faith in

Mom, Dad, Beverly, Ken (Dad pastors church)

God was genuine and unwavering. In fact, her child-like, yet mature, faith enticed me toward a relationship with God.

Chasing the American Dream

Mom was 18 and Dad was 17 when they married in 1943 in Stratford, Oklahoma. Their marriage certificate says Dad was 18, but he wasn't. He had to lie so he could get a marriage certificate without his parents signing for him. How could he get their permission? They lived 1500 miles away in California. Besides, Dad left home on bad terms; they probably would have signed nothing except a warrant for his arrest.

Soon after they married, the U.S. Army drafted Dad. He left a pregnant wife with her family in Oklahoma while he was gone. When World War II ended in 1945, my father returned home to his new bride and infant son. They moved to California so Dad might find work. Times were tough. Work was scarce. But men willing to work hard could support their families. Women stayed home, as they said, "barefoot and pregnant." They kept meals on the table, washed clothes on a scrub board, and kept popping out babies. My parents' second pregnancy ended in a stillbirth at delivery. A baby they buried without a name. Mom never talked about it, but the family knew that loss broke her and Dad's hearts.

Bobby was their firstborn. After the stillbirth of their second child, Ken came next. I was the fourth pregnancy in five years. Life was different after Bobby died. After the war, Dad had picked cotton, milked cows, drove a Coca-Cola truck, and worked in construction. But, Bobby's death must have stirred some kind of spiritual awakening in my dad. The next thing I knew, we were moving to San José, across the bay from San Francisco. Dad had become a preacher; he was going to pastor a church!

We drove up to the Pentecostal Holiness Church in San José with high hopes. Dad had bought himself a suit, tie, and white shirt. He even bought a guitar so he could lead the worship. When we arrived, we saw the front steps to the church had not been finished. So Dad built semi-circle concrete steps leading up to the church door. He seemed proud of those steps as the church people complimented him on a job well done. I was proud of him too.

It may seem strange that one could pastor a church without even a grade school education, and with little Bible training and no seminary education. But my dad must have been an imposing speaker and effective salesman who impressed people. Besides, he needed work and the church needed a pastor. I admired him for trying.

My parents had many great talents, but musical ability was not among them. To my knowledge neither of them ever played any instruments before taking on the role of accompanying congregational singing. But, it didn't matter to me; we had a small house beside the church and a predictable life for two full years. Two. Full. Years. It was heavenly. I went to Sunday School every Sunday, earning perfect attendance pins and learning memory verses every week. Good seed in good soil, Mom said.

Mom must have known the importance of memorizing Bible verses and putting His Word in your heart. Looking back, I can see how the Word of God became an anchor of moral stability which inspired me later in life to become a Sunday School teacher and even write Sunday School literature.

Looking back now as a child psychologist, I can see the hand of the Creator in my life. Just as with every infant created, He has given me unique giftings, personality traits, brain functioning, and physical traits. I so completely identify with David's heart in Psalm 139: 13-14:

> *"For you created my inmost being; you knit me together in my mother's womb. I praise you because I am fearfully and wonderfully made; your works are wonderful, I know that full well."*

Chapter 2

Invisible Girl

As I started first grade in San José, they placed me in a speech class. I was shy and didn't want anyone looking at me or talking to me. At church, people would try to get me to talk because of my drawl and poor articulation, so I would hide myself in my mother's dress. I would shriek: "Don't wook at me!" and they would howl. Why did they think that was so funny? I detested being the center of attention. My cheeks would burn hot pink with embarrassment when they teased me. I wanted to be invisible. And I certainly didn't want anyone to hear me speak.

Well, OK, there was one exception to my not wanting to be heard: my brother Ken. I tormented him with my sing-song rhymes which went on and on and on. I even made myself sick of those rhymes, but it was worth it just to get under Ken's skin. But he had other ways of getting back at me. Before the days of trampolines, we built one with an old mattress and box springs. We had the perfect setup. An old two-story shed out back of our house had a cut-out window at one end of the second story loft and a ladder at the other end. Ken and I would take turns running up the ladder, taking a flying leap out the window, and landing on the mattress springs below.

Ken and Beverly

After having enough of my torments one day, Ken planned revenge. He moved the trampoline away from the window while I climbed up the ladder. I can still feel the stinging pain in my ankles as I landed on the hardened dirt several feet below. Ken seemed to earn a good many whippings those days, but that one was a doozy. I couldn't even laugh at him because I felt sorry for his stinging bottom. I'm not sure whose body parts felt more pain, his or mine, but both of us were in tears.

While in first grade I began to catch glimpses of social differences; like, who my family was and how I compared to my schoolmates. Not only was my speech impaired, I also became distressingly aware of social prejudice, especially the reality of my parents' poverty and lack of education. They drove an old-fashioned car that clanged loudly, a sound that drew attention to the chitty-chitty-bang-bang contraption. When Dad drove us to school, I would get out of the car as quickly as I could so no one would see me. I did not want to be ridiculed.

But embarrassment became my frequent companion during those years—embarrassed by my parents, embarrassed by our poverty, embarrassed by my impaired speech. Now, looking back as a child psychologist, I have great empathy for children in poverty. I know that the same God that healed my broken spirit and helped me overcome my low self-esteem can do the same for them.

The first man to make my heart skip a beat came to our home in San José. Tall, thin, and handsome, he drove up to our home in a grey and pink Studebaker. His name was Bobby Jack Clem, and I thought I had met the love of my life. It didn't matter to me that I was 6 and he was 20 years older. I was sure he loved me as much as I loved him and he would wait for me to grow up. He stayed with us for a week while he preached a revival at our church. I followed him around like a gosling chasing its mother. A week later he left me behind for his next revival meeting. I couldn't understand why he couldn't stay with us for the next 15 years to give me time to grow up. That was my first broken heart.

On the Road Again

Although life was heavenly in San José for my mother (because of the predictable and stable life), it was not so great for my dad. I remember overhearing my parents talk about "Sister Flowers," who apparently did not appreciate my dad's ministry. It sure seemed like she was trying to get rid of the young preacher who didn't have experience pastoring a church and probably didn't even finish school. Well, she may have been right about all that, but Dad was doing his best to preach on Sundays while working odd jobs through the week. But, after two years, we left the parsonage, our stable home life, and began chasing Dad's dreams again.

Dad didn't go back to church, any church, for a long time. I was learning harsh truths, that people hurt people and that ***hurt people really hurt other people***. I was doing my best not to hurt people and, as the child "born old," to not do anything to hurt my mom and dad. They had been hurt enough by others.

Soon we were moving from place to place with a new baby sister. Carol was downright adorable! Mom molded her red hair into a Mohawk-style curl on top of her head. She dressed her in frilly dresses that stood straight out from the waist. I was glad I didn't have to wear all those silly layers of prickly can-cans. Carol knew she was cute and fully played the princess role.

Carol was the sparkle in Dad's eye. He adored her and she quickly became his favorite. Everyone knew it, but that reality brought real pain to me; I had been the only daughter in the family up until then. Dad often sat her on top of the TV and took pictures with his new 35mm camera. The camera showed up shortly after she was born, not before. I tried not to be jealous. I adored Carol like everyone else, but it was hard for me to watch her, seven years my junior, get so much attention.

During that time, Mom developed heart problems which caused her to faint frequently. No one asked me to take care of Mom or Carol, but it seemed to be the only thing to do; they both needed care and Dad was away much of the time. Knowing that Mom was fragile and weak, I worried that she might die, just like Bobby. I did my best as a 7-year-old to ease her burden by trying to take care of my newborn sister and help with household chores.

The rules of the house assigned Ken and me to wash, dry, and put the dishes away each evening. We despised it. I would rather clean toilets than wash those dishes, especially the pans. To break the boredom, we entertained ourselves with the tea towels. We learned to twist them tight and pop the other with a quick snap of the wrist. Ken made the loudest pops and the reddest marks on my legs or arms. I fought back as best I could, but he was just plain bigger and stronger than me. Then, Mom would hear our shrieks and break it up. Or, if it got really bad, she would call Dad in to settle the ordeal; neither one of us could sit down for a while after he applied his method of settling childhood squabbles.

I hoped that Mom would give up on making us wash those dirty dishes. We tried doing a bad job – leaving food on them, spilling dirty dishwater on the floor, and even breaking a dish or two. No such luck. She or Dad would call us back to the kitchen to do it right, again and again. We had to go back and "make that kitchen shine, shine, shine!" I learned to recoil at those words. But that habit stuck with me into adulthood. Even now, the last thing I do at night is to start the dishwasher and the first thing I do in the morning is unload it. I like my kitchen to "shine, shine, shine."

Route 66 Blues

After we left San José, our moves became more frequent and covered further distances. Mom's family remained in Oklahoma while most of Dad's folks had settled in California. Dad's family was trying to strike it rich in the land of opportunity. Mom didn't seem to care much about striking gold at all; she just wanted enough gold to buy food and shelter for her children. Although Mom was much more educated than Dad, she had never worked outside the home. Dad was the sole breadwinner.

The moves back and forth across the country from California to Oklahoma began when I was in third grade and continued for three years. Dad just couldn't get traction in his jobs.

In those days, traveling the historic US Route 66 from Oklahoma City to Los Angeles took you right through Needles, California. Of course, that was the path of the Joad family in Steinbeck's *The Grapes of Wrath.* That desert town of fewer than 5,000 was known for extreme heat and aridity during the summer. Summer temperatures of 120 degrees or more often set national temperature records. Even their low temperatures of the night have hit three digits. Needles holds the record for the "hottest rain" in world history: 115 degrees.

Every time we reached Needles on our trips across the country, it felt like we were passing through a lake of fire. Most cars had no air conditioning in those days. We would roll the windows down until we couldn't take the desert sandblasting our faces any more. But, rolling them up was suffocating, so we'd roll them down again. Never been so hot in my life. Little did I know then that, one day, I would be in a northern Kenyan desert on the Sudan border and would, once again, endure 100+ degree heat. Needles had helped prepare me for that desert experience 35 years earlier. I also had no idea that, one day, I would dance in the glorious desert with no thought of the temperature.

In my third, fourth, and fifth years of school, we were still making cross-country moves. On more than one occasion, Ken and I had to show up at our new school and check ourselves into the office by ourselves. Mom didn't drive a car, so when Dad was away, she had no way to take us to school. Besides, she reasoned, we had previous records at the school because we had been there before, so re-enrolling was not a big deal.

But it was a big deal for me. More than anything, I hated walking into a new classroom in the middle of a school year while 35 sets of eyes stared at the new kid. It felt like I was walking onto center stage, unprepared. I stood there in front of the room in utter stage fright. I wanted to sink into the floor and never be seen again. Were they looking at my home-made dress or well-worn shoes? Were they sizing me up, wondering if I were smart or stupid, nice or mean? I didn't know their thoughts, but I suspected the worst. I learned not to make eye contact as I made my way to the back of the classroom and slunk into the desk for yet another humiliating entry into school. *Please, God, make me invisible.*

Dad's dreaming did not stop. In fact, his dreams seemed to get bigger. They caused us to pick up and move at a moment's notice. I could hardly bear it when we had to move … again and again. Just when I made a friend at school, I had to leave. Why couldn't I have normal parents like other kids? Why couldn't I have new clothes and new shoes so I could just fit in? I felt inferior to all of them. I imagined they looked at me as a poor tall skinny kid (Ken's nickname for me was "toothpick legs") who suddenly disappears and then reappears three months later and then, poof, gone again. It's natural to suspect others are thinking badly of us when we think poorly of ourselves. Those students were probably thinking more about recess than my shoes. Social comparison took a painful toll on me.

Dad must have thought his dreams were reachable and that our moves were taking us in the direction of upward mobility. But even as a 10-year-old, I could see we were going in circles and downward. Mom never talked about it, but I knew she too was tired of chasing dreams that never materialized and always cost us money. Dad's dreams disrupted life. I don't believe I thought I was wiser than Dad, but I believed his dreams were unreachable. Why couldn't he see it?

MAN OF THE YEAR
CHRIS HARRIS, OKLAHOMA
PERSONAL SHIPMENT TOTAL...1959
$101,218.45

Man of the Year (Dad—Saladmaster's top salesman)

At one point, Mom and Dad decided it would be better for Mom and us kids to stay put in one place and let Dad move around locating work. They couldn't keep carting the whole family around the western half of the United States.

Later, Dad finally reached some of his dreams. His persistence and hard work did bring him financial success; Saladmaster's magazine proclaimed Dad "Man of the Year" with $101,000 in sales in 1959. The next year, he was named "National Salesman of the Year." Of course, we heard how Dad's demonstration of Saladmaster cookware for dinner parties was a huge hit at their national convention.

I admit I was proud of him for that. Unfortunately, the money and material possessions he sought never brought him happiness within his family relationships – at least not with his wife and, especially, not with me.

Looking back over my life I can now see more dimensions of how God formed me for my life's work. The larger issue was not my life, but His life and purpose within all of us. And the real story for my life is how His design gave me empathy for children who slip into the shadows, the gift of realizing the unpredictability of life and how suddenly it can take away loved ones, and seeing that unrealistic dreaming can be so costly, especially to children. He also let me see that being misunderstood and rejected by someone who is *supposed* to love you is one of the greatest agonies of the human heart. But, I have also learned God's love is unconditional and trustworthy, even when we feel rejected.

Chapter 3

Seized by a Great Affection

By the time I was in fifth grade, school had become a shelter for me. It was orderly and knowable; math every morning from 9:00 to 9:40, reading from 9:45 to 10:45, and recess from 10:45 to 11:00. And I thrived on it. Our home life had been chaotic and unpredictable for years. As I see now, God gave me a time of stability so I could be influenced by Freda Sauer, a teacher who would point me into a direction God had prepared for me. It took years for me to get there, but the preparation for the launch was essential for me to get ready.

When I returned from the west coast to my Oklahoma school in the middle of fifth grade, I won the lottery! Mrs. Sauer became my teacher. She remains my favorite teacher of all time because *she believed in me*. She told me I was smart and could go to college. More than that, she unlocked the power of my imagination. She filled my head with dreams of a career, like medicine, astronomy, or even modeling. Often, she would have me practice walking as a model with a book balanced on my head (a skill which later paid off at some modeling events in college). I adored her.

As this teacher put dreams and goals in my heart, my world began to expand. At first, I felt uncomfortable with these new possibilities. As my dad's daughter, dreaming had always scared me, left a bad taste in my mouth. Even though I wanted to believe Mrs. Sauer, I locked it out of my heart until much later in life when I could thoroughly examine this stuff of dreams.

My family was Protestant, Evangelical, and Pentecostal – we believed in the power of the supernatural. We believed that God didn't lie, that His Word was true, *reliable*. In Sunday School, we learned Bible verses each week; teachers taught us that God loved us no matter what, but that He wanted us to love Him and love others. I believed that too, as much as a young child can understand any of that. I also believed if God put a dream in my heart, He would bring it to pass. That was part of my spiritual awakening.

Seized by the Power of a Great Affection[2]

My first conscious encounter with God came on a Sunday morning when I was 9 years old. An evangelist preached a powerful sermon about sin separating us from God. He told us about the abundant love God has for us – so immense that His Son died for us. His words touched my tender spirit. None of my family was there that day. Mom had stayed home with some sick children; Dad was out of state as usual. But, that Sunday morning a strong magnet pulled me to the altar. It was the initiative of Almighty God, who entered my soul with a powerful explosion of His love. I confessed my sins and professed my love for Him. I was "seized by the power of a great affection" that day.

For the first time in my life, I knew beyond doubt that I was God's child and that He loved me—and would always love me! The

2 Out-of-print book title by author and pastor Gordon Cosby

encounter with Jesus that Sunday morning – being born again – steered me in a new direction. Over the years, I came to know Him as a devoted Friend – my private wellspring of joy which no one could take away from me. The inexplicable love I experienced that day became the driving force behind my decisions; it would chart the course of my life.

So, my relationship with God became deeper and richer as I learned more about the One I met at age 9. I felt He understood me. I could see His goodwill toward me was genuine. I couldn't imagine my life without our relationship. Had I been Catholic, I may have considered the nunnery for my future. Protestants had no such convent for girls like me. So, I continued my daily devotional prayers and Bible reading. I felt I had a purpose in life, though I had no idea what that might be. It didn't matter then. I just wanted to love and be loved by God, my Friend. I was not invisible to Him. I wasn't scared of what He might see in me. He knew I wasn't perfect, yet He loved me fully. I felt safe with Him. Later, I realized He had become my Soul's Companion when I was just 9 years old.

The Mystery of Marriage

As I ended fifth grade, my family stopped moving around. Dad did a lot of traveling, finding work here and there, but we settled in Oklahoma City. About that time, I began to notice some things weren't quite right about my family. Dad was gone most of the time, leaving us to fend for ourselves. Mom still didn't drive a car. That left Ken and me to walk to the nearest grocery store with a list and all the money Mom could scrape together. Some of the cash came from the sofa cracks after visitors left. Mom also took in laundry to earn money. I knew Dad sent us as much as he could, but feeding the five of us was difficult. It seemed that we ate a lot of soup, the off-brand, cheap kind, as well as beans with cornbread.

I also began to put two and two together regarding my parents. I'd heard that opposites attract, but they were *so different* I couldn't imagine what attracted them to each other. Dad was vibrant and gregarious; he never met a stranger. Mom was soft-spoken and timid. How they got together was a mystery to me. That was when I began to understand more of Mom's heart condition and its dark possibilities. What would happen to us if Mom died while Dad was out of town?

One Sunday morning before I started sixth grade, Mom woke me about 6:00 a.m. She and Dad were on their way to the hospital to deliver their next baby. But first she wanted to tell me about puberty! Once my mind cleared and I realized what she was talking about and that she was in labor, I told her to please go on to the hospital. What a time to tell me about that kind of thing. I told her she could talk to me later if she wanted, but I already knew all about it. So, they left in a hurry. Mom was known for delivering babies fast; I myself was born on a fast-moving gurney outside the hospital. I knew Mom needed to get to the hospital before she delivered that baby on my bed!

We soon got the call: I had a brother, Christopher Dale Harris. He and I came to adore each other. At 11 years older, I claimed him as my baby boy.

Finding New Rhythms of Life

Sixth grade was a good year for me. I stayed in one school the whole year! Dad was traveling three or four months at a time, selling cookware in Montana and across the Dakotas. It certainly seemed he had found his niche. He was a born salesman. I knew he was good at it because of that cover story about him—"National Salesman of the Year"—in Saladmaster Corporation's magazine. Dad was earning more money then but Mom still took in laundry to supplement our daily needs. She taught me how to iron men's shirts, so heavily starched they could stand up without a hanger. That skill never earned me any money, but it was good to have in my back pocket just in case times got hard.

Change began rolling into my life when, in 1960, I became aware of a young man named John F. Kennedy. He was running for president against Richard Nixon. I lived in a Republican state and had a Republican family, so naturally I wanted Nixon to win. But the main reason I supported Nixon was that Kennedy was a Roman Catholic. My Protestant family strongly opposed Kennedy for that reason, and so did I. Confident that Nixon would win, I went to bed that Tuesday night, November 8, 1960, pretty darn sure that we would wake up to another Republican president.

The news the next morning shocked half of America—the half that included the Harris family. Kennedy, so young in his 40s, had barely, and I mean barely, won the election. After the jolt of electing a Catholic president had worn off, we settled in to get to know this nice-looking man from Massachusetts who put *r's* on ends of words that didn't have any and he left r's out of words that did. He sounded intelligent, so I couldn't understand why he would mix up his *r's* so badly. "You can't pahk a cah in Cuber faaa all the trahsh." But, when he stood firm during some kind of missile crisis with Cuba, he made me feel safe. Naturally, I could not know then that I would one day come to a special appreciation for the Roman Catholic Church. Their grand history, deep devotion, and rich liturgies helped deepen my faith in Jesus Christ, my Soul Companion.

In the sixth grade, our teacher required us to make a speech in front of the whole class. When Mr. Lesley called on me, I stood up and froze. Literally, just stood there and said nothing. He told me to go ahead. But, when I opened my mouth, I started laughing. And laughing that hard brings an urge to go to the bathroom. I was too afraid to ask for that privilege so I just crossed my legs and hoped for the best. He told me to sit down and he would come back to me. The class knew I was a good student, and they had never seen me so nervous like that. Neither had I! I tried to talk straight and tough to myself, "Get a hold of yourself, Beverly. Just stand up and say the stupid speech and sit down. That's all you have to do."

When my turn came around again, the same thing happened. More nervous laughter and talking very sternly to myself. Finally, I told Mr. Lesley, "Sorry. I can't do it. Just give me a zero." He looked at me like I had lost my mind. "You are really going to take a zero on this assignment? I see you have it ready. Just read it to us." "Sorry, I just can't do it." So, Mr. Lesley took my paper, read it to the class, and laughed all the way through it. He said it was hysterical. I took the zero and hurried off to the bathroom when the bell rang.

Looking back, the terror of public speaking continued to plague me through college and into grad school. Of course, I was forced to do it or I would have flunked out of school. To hide my flushed neck and dripping sweat when required to give a speech, I learned to wear a turtle-neck blouse with long sleeves and a jacket. After each oral presentation, it took several minutes to regain my composure.

But, as the years went by, I began to gain more and more confidence. Decades later, when I was called upon to speak for the needs and rights of children, the terror disappeared. Now when I am subpoenaed to testify in court for a child in foster care, my voice is strong. I have no hesitancy speaking when it comes to cruelty and injustice perpetrated on children. But finding my voice has been a miracle of God's transformation.

In the spring of sixth grade, Dad came home from one of his long trips pulling a horse trailer. We all went screaming out the front door, wondering what in the world Dad had brought us. He always brought something for Carol, something special he picked up just for her. A necklace, little princess dress, or something.

But this gift was for Ken, not Carol. A palomino horse from Montana. When a new customer couldn't afford a set of Dad's cookware, he took the horse in exchange. Dad believed in his stainless-steel cookware so much, that he would sometimes give away sets to people who couldn't afford them. The horse was not a bad swap, except we lived in the suburbs. The backyard of our 1100-square-foot house was just not big enough for a horse. To keep "Montana" in our yard, we had to tie him to a clothesline post. When the poor thing was clearly terrified and tried to escape, Dad found a place about a mile from our house to corral him. Even though Ken was scared of Montana, he walked the mile most days to care for the horse. After all, the horse was a gift from his dad.

Ken adored Dad. Carol adored him too. Chris was just a wee thing, but he squealed with delight when Dad came home from his travels. Dad was full of life and fun when he came home. He brought gifts and entertained us with stories of his life on the road. Everyone seemed to adore Dad.

Except me.

I kept my distance. He was my dad and I knew I was supposed to respect him, but I couldn't trust him. I had seen him get angry with Mom. I heard them arguing at night. And I didn't like the way he barked orders at Mom about fixing a meal or cleaning his shoes. I saw his impatience with me when I wanted his attention. I had hoped that being a good student would make him proud of me. But, when I tried to show him my report card, he shoved me away. I went to my bedroom, doubled over in pain. Loving my daddy became harder and harder for me. I stayed in my bedroom much of the time when Dad was home.

One night I awakened to the sounds of Mom and Dad arguing, screaming actually, in the hallway outside my open bedroom door. Suddenly, Mom fainted. I jumped from my bed to help her. As Dad picked her up, I lost it! I screamed, "Leave her alone. I hate you. I hate you. You killed my mama." Dad was shocked. So was I. But it was honest.

Dad carried her to their bed. I grabbed a wet cloth and soon she came back to consciousness. He had not killed her, just killed her spirit, her happiness. What kind of man would do that to a stranger, much less his wife?

I later understood that in that moment, I was actually railing against the bad things in his life—his unfaithfulness to Mom, his dishonesty with merchants, and his concealing bad habits. My siblings didn't know about those things and I dared not tell them. I never told Mom about the lipstick I had seen on his white collar when I was doing laundry (she never wore lipstick). So, my hatred that spewed out in that moment was more than his rejection of me; it was the cry from a daughter who had lost all respect for her father because of his hypocrisy. No one knew about those secret sins except me. If Mom knew, she never spoke of it. But, God knew and it crushed me that Dad would do such horrible things to people he was supposed to love. Why was he two-faced?

The Day My World Changed

On April 12, 1961, Dad became ill on the road. He was hospitalized in Mangum, a small town in southern Oklahoma (thank God he was not up north in Montana or the Dakotas). A friend drove Mom down to check on him. She called that night to assure us Dad would be fine.

We expected Mom to bring Dad home the next day. The next morning, we all sat around the table eating the breakfast Aunt Lorene had prepared for us. Carol, Ken, and I prepared to head out the door for school. When the phone rang at 7:00 a.m., Aunt Lorene answered the call that changed our family forever.

"Hello. How's Chris? ... you don't mean it... children, your daddy is dead... did he make things right with God? ... oh, thank God!" Click.

Ken never heard another word past "dead." He jumped up and started screaming, "No, no, no! It can't be! No, please God, No!"

In a stupor, I got up from the table and went straight to the bathroom. No tears. No sounds. I began cleaning the sink, the bathtub, the toilet, the floor. Finally, when I had gained control over that tiny space, I sat on the toilet seat in a daze. And I talked to my Soul Companion. "Oh, God. Oh, God. Help us. What will happen to us? How can Mom take care of us? Oh, God, come to our assistance. We need help!" The only consolation I had in that moment was that Dad had made peace with God before his death. But his peace with God did not reach the shores of my heart for a few more decades.

Ever since Mom started having heart problems, I thought she would die first, leaving us with Dad. I couldn't comprehend what life would be like without Dad. Even though I had no confidence in his parenting and caring for us if Mom died first, he was still the strongest person I ever knew. Now, our sole breadwinner was gone. Forever gone. Although my world was caving in, I had a strong sense we would be OK. It would take a while, but we would get back to normal. I wasn't sad. Or angry. Or happy. If I felt anything, it was relief; we would not be moving around anymore. He would not hurt Mom anymore. He would not cheat and steal any more. But who could feed and care for us? Mom couldn't even drive a car.

I did not shed tears for my dad for another 37 years. I may have only been 12 years old, but I felt the weight of two young children. Our

Carol, Beverly, Chris, and Ken (4 siblings left after Dad's death)

ship was pitching and rolling, but I didn't fall overboard; ropes lashed me to the mast.

I missed school that day. Later that afternoon, a car pulled up outside – Uncle Carl and Aunt Rachel were visiting from California and just happened to drop by on that day. At 26, Carl was nine years younger than Dad, and the spitting image of him. Even their voices sounded the same.

That evening, the air was so dense in our house that I found it hard to breathe. Voices were low and despondent. Just when I felt I couldn't take any more of the heaviness, Aunt Rachel came bouncing through the house on a broomstick with a stringed mop on her head—laughing and carrying on like she was at a circus. Everybody looked in disbelief at the disrespect for the bereaved. But it was just what everyone in that house needed. Our family was not going down into the grave with my dad. We would make it; we would be OK. It might take a while, and some of Dad's brothers might need to help Mom get on her feet, but this family of four kids and a single mom would survive. I also knew that Aunt Lorene and Uncle Leon would not let us drown in those swirling waters of gloom.

The weight of Dad's death lifted. At least for a moment. But it brought just enough perspective to let me see a flicker of the sun behind those black thunderheads. I felt hope for the first time since the phone call. I felt it, even if no one else did.

After the funeral, I tried to get a grip on my emotions so that I could go on with life. I felt no sadness, but I was downright angry with Dad. I may have felt I owed it to Mom to be angry with the way he treated her. And I felt such disgust with his secret sins. If I forgave him, wouldn't that send a message to Mom that hurting her was OK? If I grieved over him, I would be taking his side against her and minimizing his hypocrisy. I wanted to be loyal to my mother because she didn't deserve the hard knocks that hit her in life. In a way I didn't understand at the time, I was also angry with Dad for dying, leaving Mom to raise four kids by herself. That anger stayed with me for decades. At the time, I didn't know anger can be such a strong grieving emotion. I also knew that Ken, Carol, and Chris were heartbroken by his death and I did my best to comfort them. I never let them know how I felt about Dad or what I knew about his hypocritical lifestyle.

During that time of harboring anger and resentment toward my dad, my heart became hard as concrete toward him. It would take dynamite to break it up. The destructiveness within us can seldom be transformed until we confront it ourselves. No one can do it for us. That confrontation often leads us to the pit where the demons dwell. Despair must set in before we are ready to face those demons. But, when I finally did confront my own monsters almost four decades later, the dynamite blast broke up the hardness of heart and changed my life forever.

After Mom took care of all the funeral expenses and paperwork, she had to learn to drive. How Mom passed her driving test—at age 35— is beyond me. When she started driving, she didn't have to tell us kids to be quiet so she could concentrate on the road. We were all scared spitless. We took shallow breaths and didn't make a peep when she was behind the wheel.

With my father no longer around and with Mom's full plate of responsibilities, I could have lost my direction and even my life in that desert place. But I firmly believe my Soul Companion placed other family and friends in my life to help keep me on track.

Chapter 4

Hitting the Jackpot

After my father's death when I was 12, I withstood a test of endurance which lasted until I was 18. Although I still lived at home, I felt I was expected to take care of myself and be fully responsible for my actions and decisions. I suppose I had freedom to be wild and get into mischief, but I had no desire to do that. I wanted to do what was right, if for no other reason than to respect my mother and love God my Father.

Life's New Shapes and Sounds

Two summers after Dad died, Mom surprised us by announcing we would drive to California for a vacation. We planned to stay a couple of weeks with Dad's brothers in Sacramento and visit Grandma Harris in Los Angeles.

When we rode back and forth between California and Oklahoma while Dad was driving, we almost never stopped at a motel. We might pull off for Dad to sleep a bit, but then kept it moving. But Mom didn't have that kind of stamina. I was glad she didn't because it was scary enough to ride with her in broad daylight. It wasn't that she was a wild driver. Not at all. In fact, that was the problem; Mom was a timid driver. She never passed anyone. Not even a farmer on a tractor. I knew it would take us a long time to get to California at her speed.

We spent our second night in Winslow, Arizona. After checking out of the motel that morning, Mom decided to let Ken drive. He had been itching to drive since he had received his driver's license three weeks earlier. She thought it was safe since that part of Arizona was not known for heavy traffic. Mom sat in the front passenger seat with 3-year-old Chris beside her. Carol and I sat in the back seat.

Ken, who believed in "pedal to the medal," had only driven a few miles when our car started pitching and lurching up and down and turning sideways. Mom's door flew open. She and Chris slid out and landed on huge rocks. Carol and I screamed in horror. Ken, petrified, brought the car to a stop. Apparently, he had been gazing off at mountains in the distance and drifted off the road.

Ken jumped out and ran back to Mom and Chris. Her leg was badly slashed and scraped and Chris had a gash in his head. In the backseat, the floor buckled up beneath my feet. A passerby stopped and helped get Mom and Chris back in the car. He told us of a hospital back in Winslow. Ken turned the car around and sped back. I yelled at him to slow down! As we flew down the road, I prayed, "Please, please, dear God, help us get to the hospital without another wreck and please, please don't let my mama die."

The hospital admitted Mom and Chris. Her leg required many stitches. We called Uncle John in Sacramento. He told us to stay right there; he would get there the next day. The next morning, our uncles John and Paul arrived at the motel, having driven 13 hours through the night. They took us to breakfast. I was so relieved to see these two angels who had come to rescue us; I felt safe again with two experienced drivers. Our two-week vacation in California turned out to be eight weeks so mom's leg could heal. I think we all heaved a collective sigh of relief when we pulled up in our driveway in Oklahoma at the end of the summer. That was the last time our family went to California for a vacation. No one ever mentioned going again—it was too risky.

Hitting the Jackpot

We lived in one of the best school districts in the state of Oklahoma (or so the state rankings told us), but I dreaded starting high school. It was huge, with more than 3,000 students. I felt I could hold my own academically, but I also knew I had some strikes against me.

Strike one—I was still painfully shy, so making friends was hard. Strike two—I came from a poor family, so I couldn't participate in any extra-curricular activities. Strike three—with no dad in the family and with two younger siblings, I felt responsible for helping Mom with laundry, meals, and getting kids to bed. Thankfully, we were given a small monthly income from Social Security because of Dad's military service. It covered food and housing expenses. But, I felt I needed to earn extra money to buy my own clothes and some for Carol.

That's why I was surprised when Mom talked to Ken and me about going to nearby Southwestern, a private Christian high school. When I asked how we could afford it, Mom said she could get a job at Southwestern in exchange for our tuition. She would only have to work during school hours so she could be at home when we came in from school. I asked no more questions. I think Mom was afraid we would not want to leave the stable school environment of the past three years. But that news thrilled me. I could attend a small school where I could take Bible classes every day. Sweet!

My 16th birthday was the most memorable of my growing up years. That morning, Mom drove me to downtown Oklahoma City to get my driver's license. Uncle Leon had taught me to drive defensively, parallel park, and do turnarounds safely. The driving test that day was extensive, requiring all those skills and many more. Mom seemed proud of me for getting my license when I was 16; she got hers at age 35 and even then, she was never a confident driver. Mom also threw a surprise birthday party for me later that afternoon after I got home from work. Since I had never had a birthday party at all, it was a shocker, with a house full of my friends, a cake, and a record player of my very own. Someone bought me a 45rpm Beatles record (after all, the year was 1964). I received another gift of a four-inch plastic doll of the Beatles' drummer Ringo Starr. I've kept that image of Ringo for 55 years now; it's still in mint condition. Like I said, it was an unforgettable birthday which my mother made happen.

In my junior year of high school, my mother remarried. And, she and her new husband along with 9-year-old Carol and 5-year-old Chris were going to move to Ardmore in southern Oklahoma, where they would pastor a church. I really didn't want to leave my Christian high school because I was thriving. Chess club. Band. Boyfriends. Popular. Well, popular as a "nerd." I didn't care; I loved learning and reading.

I'm not sure how it happened, but Mom agreed for Ken and me to remain in Oklahoma City to finish high school at Southwestern while she moved 100 miles away. Perhaps mom felt relieved of two teenagers who may not have been thrilled with their new stepfather. But, as for me, I felt free to work hard in school and help support myself. I would need scholarships to get through college. I would tell my mother about it after I got accepted. That was the plan.

Mom's health had not improved much, so having a husband share the responsibility of child care of younger children probably felt more secure for her. My thoughts were different; I felt mom deserved to be loved and cared for more than my dad had shown her. I hoped her new husband would give her that.

When Mom and my stepdad moved to Ardmore, Oklahoma, Ken moved into the dormitory on the Southwestern campus to finish his last year of school. I moved in with my Aunt Lorene and Uncle Leon. They had been a stable rock of security throughout my life. They had taken us to church and other places when Dad was on the road. They were at our home when Mom brought our baby brother Chris home from the hospital, and they were with us the morning we learned about Dad's death. They were as close to me as any parents could be. Looking back now, I realize that moving in with the Crosswhites formed another phase of my move toward independence.

So, there I was at age 16, living with my cousin, aunt, and uncle, whom I adored. I hit the jackpot! I was no longer responsible for preparing meals, doing the laundry, trying to corral my younger

Leon and Lorene Crosswhite (aunt and uncle)

siblings, or worrying about Mom's health. For the first time in my life, I could be a normal kid, whatever that meant. My cousin Jan and I became like sisters during those two years we lived together. Heaven had surely arrived on earth!

Life in that home was strict and structured. A knock on our bedroom door at 6:00 a.m. sharp signaled time to rise, make the bed, get dressed, and be at the breakfast table at 6:20. Finish at 6:35, brush teeth, and walk out the front door at 6:45 to arrive at school after a 10-minute walk. Be in your first period seat by 7:00 a.m. Sharp.

Uncle Leon worked as an efficiency expert at Tinker Air Force Base. When he informed me that my curfew was 10:00 p.m., he meant I had to be inside the house with the front door closed by the 10th dong of the grandfather clock. One second later would ground me the next weekend. I had never had curfew before, so I really didn't understand why precision was so important. After testing his rules, I learned he meant what he said. It wasn't personal. It was just expected if I wanted to be part of their family. And I did. Life at my mom's home had not been rigid at all, but because I had so much responsibility as the older daughter, I was the one setting the limits for my younger siblings.

Because I had lived in two very different homes growing up, I could see clearly how a structured routine, consistent rules, and high expectations were better. In the Crosswhite home, I learned how to respect a spouse, invest in your children, and show hospitality. And – have fun! Lorene kept a meticulous home, always had homemade desserts for family and drop-ins, and made sure there were fresh-cut bouquets from her flower garden on the coffee table. She was Martha Stewart before Martha knew how to turn on the oven. Lorene and Leon were fun-loving and God-fearing and made life simple and enjoyable. It was the kind of home environment I wanted when I started my own life.

Looking back, I can see additional preparation for my life journey while a student at Southwestern High School. I had developed close personal relationships with several faculty members. I had been the babysitter for several families, including those of my high school teachers Lavoy Hatchett and Franklin Sexton. I enjoyed close ties with the families of Southwestern's president, Dr. W. R. Corvin, and Vice President and Dean, Dr. Harold Paul. Those educators not only held high positions of leadership in Southwestern, but also in my church and community.

My insider view of these families allowed me to observe their intimate relationships with one other. Back then, I wasn't even aware that I had adopted some of their habits and traits. For example, the Sexton family always held hands together during their meal-time prayers. I carried that tradition into my own family after my marriage. Thus, my relationship with God was being grounded in beautiful and valuable ways.

At Southwestern High School I was required to attend chapel three times a week and take daily Bible classes with an inspirational teacher, M.W. Murr. During my four years there, the intense Bible studies took me through the entirety of the Holy Scripture.

While some of my friends at Southwestern planned weddings after high school graduation, I had no such intention. I had dated several guys but not for long. I knew I was headed to college. When I eventually talked to Mom about going to college, she asked good questions: Which college? How would I get there? Would I need a car? How would I pay for everything?

I had worked and saved as much as I could since I was 12 years old. Still, I knew $200 wouldn't get far in college. I told Mom not to worry about it, that I would figure it out myself. And I did. Two of my high school teachers secured teaching positions at Oral Roberts

University, which had opened in Tulsa the year before I graduated. They encouraged me to apply and said they would help me get scholarships. Because I had graduated top of my class and scored well on the national entrance exam into colleges, they believed they could get most of my expenses covered. I did as they suggested, and before I knew it, ORU accepted me.

When I told Mom about it, she wasn't as excited as I thought she would be. She lived by the maxim: "Expect nothing and you'll never be disappointed." I think she thought I might be setting myself up for disappointment if I entered college and either didn't succeed or couldn't pay for it and had to drop out. My stepfather didn't want me to go at all. He simply misunderstood why I wanted to go. Although he had sent two of his daughters to college, they both dropped out to get married. So, of course, for him, going to college was a waste. He couldn't see he got anything for his money. He told me, "All you want is an MRS degree and you don't need to go to college to get that." He did me a great favor with that statement. If I would ever even think about dropping out of college, his statement would keep me going.

So, with the guidance of friends and personality traits from my family, I passed the test of being an autonomous adolescent and was ready to be launched into adulthood. Or, at least I thought I was. And that gave me enough confidence to get started on the journey.

Chapter 5

Go, Go! Don't Look Back!

No one in my immediate family had gone to college, but I had heard a voice from God. It was like I had been trapped in a mine collapse when the rocks suddenly shifted, opening a path up to the clear air. God gave me education as my tunnel to the top. It was like He kept saying, "Go. Go. Forget the fears. Just go. Get out quick! I'll show you the way. Don't look back. I'll be with you."

Without those words from Mrs. Sauer in the fifth grade encouraging me onward to college and God showing me the path out of the abyss, I'm sure my life would have languished. Looking back over my life, I see that God, in Peter's words, brought me up "out of darkness into His marvelous light."[3] His light eventually led me to a life of service—a call to help widows and orphans, victims and perpetrators, the defenseless and the disenfranchised, the deserving and the

3 1 Peter 2:9 taken from the NEW AMERICAN STANDARD (NAS): Scripture taken from the NEW AMERICAN STANDARD BIBLE®, copyright© 1960, 1962, 1963, 1968, 1971, 1972, 1973, 1975, 1977, 1995 by The Lockman Foundation. Used by permission.

undeserving, and those with chemical addictions and sexual perversions to discover God's unfathomable love for them.

And I flew up the underground path, away from the impoverishment and limitations of my genes and circumstances. But, despite those limitations, I learned perseverance from all the role models in my family. Giving up was not an option.

In our western culture, 18 seems to represent the age of independence, freedom from restraint, the time to move into the indulgences of the wide-open spaces of adulthood. Those new adults can finally drink, smoke, frolic in immorality, join the military, and maybe run away with the circus. For me, age 18 was just another mile-marker along the path that led from the mine collapse to fresh air; it marked the remaining distance to college. I graduated from high school in May, 1966, just before I turned 18 in June. I moved home for the summer to be with my mother before leaving for college in the fall.

Tulsa

In September 1966, Mom bought me a one-way bus ticket to Tulsa, put me on the big Greyhound with my two suitcases, and waved good-bye. She didn't cry. I didn't either, not until we were way down the road and no one could see. I allowed the tears to flow silently as I navigated the emotions of leaving one life behind before clearly seeing the next one. After a few hours of traveling Oklahoma highways, we finally arrived at the Tulsa bus station. I had a dime in my pocket to call the college from a pay phone.

Thank God, they were expecting me. Soon, someone from ORU whisked me and my luggage away into my big new adventure. I only knew two teachers, including the one who gave me the job in the math department. Both Lavoy Hatchett and Franklin Sexton believed in me, and both of their wives had been my role models. I felt so lonely, arriving in a large city with all the unknowns lurking out there in front of me. Mom had promised to write and send me $5 a week. My stepdad told me not to call collect and rack up a big phone bill unless I faced an emergency. I felt certain I could not count on him for anything. And I also knew that Mom could never stand up for me. She loved me, but, like many women, she feared crossing any man who had power over her.

Somewhere along the way, I vowed *never* to fall into that trap as an adult. I would make sure I could support myself financially. And I would teach my children to be independent. I didn't want them to suffer the hardship of feeling trapped with no way out.

I felt pressure; I had to make a high GPA to maintain my scholarships, and I had to work 20 hours a week as part of my room and board. But I was motivated on several levels. I had to prove Mrs. Sauer right and my stepdad wrong. I also had to show myself that hard work could pay off. And I felt a compulsion to make the world a better place, simply because I was born and lived in it. I needed to cooperate with God in His plan for my life, whatever it was. That's probably why I carried an overload of courses. I was there for an education, not partying.

No roommate showed up, so I had a private room. Sweet! I could take my early morning classes, work in the afternoon, go to the library, and stay up late preparing for the next day's classes. But a few weeks later, a roommate moved in. She had already gone through two other roommates. Failing to get along with them, they moved her into my room. She took only a minimum of coursework, had no work responsibilities, and was a spoiled brat. She also was one moody girl who had frequent migraines. When she had a headache, all the lights in the room had to be off and I had to tiptoe out the door so I wouldn't disturb the princess.

Paul Oxley

But, isn't that part of why we go to college? We have to learn to work with difficult people. One day, I saw her wearing one of my shirts on campus. She had a wardrobe that shouted "Vogue," and mine whispered, "Thrift store." When she saw my displeasure at her wearing my clothes, she said, "Mine are all dirty. I didn't think you'd mind." In time, I learned to really like her. When she was in a good mood, we enjoyed deep belly laughs about ridiculous things.

A Man Named Paul

I met a seminarian my freshman year. He was one of the teaching assistants in a large Old Testament Survey class. For reasons known only to my heart, I worked hard to impress him. But he was not so easily impressed. That only made me work harder to turn his eye.

Unfortunately, I had swimming class immediately prior to his Old Testament class, which meant I had to go to class with wet hair. Some girls look cute with curly wet hair. I was not one of them. My hair was long and straggly; I looked like a drowned Lhasa Apso. In time, I noticed he didn't seem to mind my unkempt appearance.

I had developed a reputation for being a cold fish since I showed little affection to young men. I was not cold, but selective. I had learned that men had a dark side: they could become animals. I didn't want to make the same mistakes as my mother. So, I was cautious. Years later, a therapist helped me work through my bad experiences of degenerate men during my childhood.

But Paul Oxley was different. He was a good guitarist, highly intelligent, and very respectful to women. His baby blue eyes melted my heart. Paul also worked as the library checker, the one who sat at the library exit to make sure no students took books without proper check-out. I devised a plan to get his attention. I would 'steal' one of the books from the library, so he would catch my theft. Then, I would feign surprise and go check it out properly. But, to my disappointment, he didn't detect my theft. So, I walked out, then immediately walked back in and told him of his sloppy work as library checker. He was not moved in the least. "Well, if you want to steal a book, I can't stop you, but you will have to answer to God for it, for He knows all."

I was stricken. Not only did I fail to get his attention, but now I was on his black list of thieves.

I continued enrolling in Paul's classes; I had to have a platform from which to undo my bad reputation. Paul was impressive; his intense devotion to God was rock-solid and his character was impeccable. People who knew him at ORU held him in high esteem. I knew I could trust him with my innermost thoughts, my soul, my body. I knew he would never violate his vows—to me or anyone. I knew if he were to ask me for a date, it would mean he was interested in me. He didn't casually go out with girls.

In the spring of my freshman year, Paul invited me to attend a Toastmaster's International dinner where his quartet "The Friars Four" provided entertainment. After the dinner, he kissed my cheek as he walked me back to the dorm. He either forgave or forgot my book theft. Either way, I was back in his good graces by the end of the school year.

I returned to ORU for my second year in a confused state. I was interested in psychology, but the road to clinical psychology was long and demanding. I felt the need to get a degree that would bring financial security, and quickly. So, I continued to study as an undeclared major. Paul and I continued to date.

By the middle of my sophomore year of college, I was enamored with this unusual man of integrity. I had never met a guy even close to his quality in my 18 years. Then he invited me to his parents' home in Independence, Kansas for a weekend. To protect any possible smearing of my reputation, he invited one of his seminary buddies to accompany us.

Julia and Paul Oxley, Sr. were unpretentious and honest people with a heart for God's work and His children. Julia worked in a nursing home, providing meals for the patrons. Paul Sr. had pastored churches in Missouri and Kansas for almost 45 years. Because many of the churches were small, he supplemented the family income by painting and wallpapering homes.

Paul Sr. and Julia Oxley (Paul's parents)

One thing I learned about "Dad Oxley" was his scrupulous record-keeping for his tithing. In that time and economy, many people had to barter garden goods for his service. Paul Jr. showed me one of his dad's accounting books; he had listed each of the vegetables and fruits given in one column, the monetary value of each in the next column, and the tithes due in the third column. I could see that honesty and principled business practices passed down through the genes of that honorable family.

At the end of my second year of college, Paul graduated from seminary. He and four other seminarians had been offered sponsorships from ORU to do mission work for a year in East Africa. We had initially planned to marry and go to Africa together as missionaries. In fact, we had gone through the entire series of inoculations in preparation for living abroad. However, at the last minute we both felt

God telling us that only Paul should go to Africa. Marriage could wait. Frankly, I felt I needed to finish college before we took that step.

With Paul gone to Africa, I began to feel the need to move home to be with my mother. I could attend East Central State University, a public college about 70 miles from Ardmore.

Life is what happens while we're making other plans

That sudden turn into new waters made no sense. Why would I give up a scholarship where I was getting a great education? Why would I return home to live with my mother, my younger siblings, and a stepfather who would be challenging for me to stay with? I didn't know why, but I knew I had to go back. I had not lived with my mother for four years, and I knew she was not well.

So, in the fall I enrolled in East Central State University and declared a major in education. I had no real choice in a major; it was the only thing I could do to finish up school on time and have a marketable degree upon graduation.

Paul returned from Uganda the following summer. When we reconnected after a year's absence, we knew we were ready to make a lifelong commitment to one another. We set a wedding date of September 5, 1969. The plan was to marry, finish up my student teaching, graduate in December, then Paul would enter a PhD program at the University of Iowa in the fall of 1970. That was the plan. But John Lennon was right: Life is what happens while we're making other plans.

My stepdad turned on the light in my bedroom at three o'clock in the morning, frantically shouting, "Call 911... your mom's not breathing!"

In a daze, I jumped from my bed and ran into mom's bedroom. My stepfather was doing CPR on her. I called 911. By then, Chris and

Carol were awake and clinging to me, crying. I thought the ambulance would never come; I went out on the front porch several times, praying for them to hurry. When they arrived, they continued CPR as they carried her to the ambulance. My stepfather went with them and told me to call some friends from our church. I also called my Aunt Lorene and Uncle Leon, who were leaving early that morning for a trip. I knew I had to stop them.

Chris and Carol were in shock. "Please, Beverly, tell us she will be OK." But I somehow knew she was going to die. I just knew. I told them, "No matter what happens, you will be OK. I'll be here with you. And God is with us. He will take care of us."

I called friends from the church who rushed over to drive us to the hospital. As we waited for news, my mind drifted back to the day before. Mom had been on bed rest for a few days. I served her hot chicken soup and light refreshments on her fine china and silver platter. I cut a red rose from the garden and placed it in a crystal vase. Then, I sat on the edge of her bed as she ate meager portions. She asked me about the wedding which was coming up in a few days. I assured her everything was prepared because it would be a simple wedding with modest décor and reception. She seemed relieved that she was not responsible for any of it. I knew she liked Paul. She had told me, "Beverly, you've had many suitors, but you have saved yourself for Paul. He is a good man and I think you will be happy with him. He will be faithful to you." Was she comparing him to my dad? I didn't know, but I knew she was right. He would be faithful to me.

I looked at a calendar on the hospital wall: August 25, 1969, just 10 days before my wedding date.

My stepfather finally walked through the doors of the hospital emergency room. He looked at me and shook his head. Grief was written all over his face. He simply said, "That's two wives I've lost." I gathered Carol and Chris in my arms and we all wept together. They were petrified. Who would care for them? At 14 and 10, they had lost both parents. They were orphans.

Naturally, the next few days were filled with making funeral arrangements. And we were trying to locate Ken. Soon after high school graduation, he had joined the Air Force. Like thousands of other American boys, the military shipped him to Vietnam. At the time Mom died, Ken was working away from his base on a mountain in a very remote part of Thailand. As a consummate techie, he formed part of an advanced effort to electronically monitor enemy troop movements. It took a couple days for the Red Cross to locate him on the mountain in Thailand.

His master sergeant woke Ken and told him he had to get off the mountain because of an emergency back home. All his gear remained at his home base when he was pulled into a helicopter and flown through heavy fog to an airbase in Vietnam.

When Ken finally walked into the living room of our home in Ardmore days later, he was still wearing his military fatigues, boots, and gun belt, minus the weapons and bullets. Bearing the stench of war, this stranger, my brother, stood at the end of the room and stared at his family. He was in as much shock as we were.

Paul and I postponed our wedding. My siblings needed me more than I needed to be married. That could wait. On the day of Mom's funeral, Paul told me that he was so glad I had moved home to be with my mother the last year of her life, rather than to go to Africa with him. I shudder to think what Carol and Chris would have faced had I not been there in the wee hours of the night when she died. God planned for me to be there in Ardmore with my family when we needed each other the most.

Love and Marriage

Paul and I married six weeks later on October 3, 1969. A very simple wedding. An elaborate wedding on the heels of Mom's death didn't seem appropriate or necessary. Chris and Carol needed security and stability, and I intended to provide it. My aunt and uncle, Leon and Lorene Crosswhite, stepped in as surrogate parents at my wedding. My cousin Janice served as matron of honor, and Paul's brother David was best man and soloist. Carol kept the guest book and Chris lit the candles. Paul's dad and my stepdad performed the ceremony. The ladies of the church provided a modest reception. My dress was borrowed.

Paul and Beverly

Four months after Mom died, my stepfather asked if Chris and Carol could stay with us for a few days. He traveled to Missouri and returned with a new bride. "Merry Christmas, kids! Meet Margie."

I was a new wife and a new teacher, 21 years old, and caring deeply for my siblings. What would happen to them? Each time they came to our small apartment, they cried for Mom. We all cried for her. She had been the pillar of the family after Dad's sudden death nine years before. Now, that pillar had collapsed, and the home structure was caving in. I knew we could not last long in that state of emotional devastation.

Beverly and 2nd grade Special Education class

Paul and I decided to remain in Ardmore for the kids until school was out in the summer. At that point, we would make decisions for our future as well as for Carol and Chris.

So, in the spring semester of 1970, I took a temporary teaching position in a second grade special education class in Ardmore. In the meantime, Carol and Chris lived with their stepdad and his new wife. I was close by.

I had my hands full with 20 special needs children in second grade; I had no support staff. The very first day I became a teacher, I had butterflies in my stomach, but I wasn't the only one. Poor Mikey threw up all over the floor as he came into his new teacher's classroom. I ran to the bathroom and grabbed as many paper towels as I could handle. As I was mopping up the vomit dressed in my 4-inch heels and mini-skirt, Mrs. Abrams came into the room and saw me on the floor. That African-American veteran teacher was the voice of reason for me that spring semester of my first year of teaching. How I adored her!

She said, "Mrs. Oxley, what are you doing on the floor?" I explained that I was cleaning up vomit. In her perfect African-American drawl, she said, "Yes, I see that, honey. But, we have custodians for that! Now get up off that floor!"

"We do?" She shook her head and mumbled as she walked out the door to go find the custodian for some naïve young teacher who knew nothing about how schools work. I learned to rely much on that wise teacher who was nearing retirement. I wanted to become just like her one day.

I taught 17 African-Americans, two white, and one American Indian student that spring. As part of the end-of-year tests in April, I gave a spelling test to my students. My instructions for the test were, "Say the spelling word once, use it in a sentence, then say it again." When I said the word "draws," 17 of the children burst out laughing. I had no idea what was going on.

At recess, I told Mrs. Abrams about the strange behavior of my class. Her laughter exploded: "Honey, don't you put on your draws when you get dressed in the morning?" I realized I had a lot to learn. My white culture had not taught me enough for what lay ahead.

In June, 1970 my stepfather and his new bride told us they were moving to another state to pastor a church. They wanted to take Chris and Carol with them. *My* siblings! That was absurd. We had to come up with a plan quickly.

After a brief discussion, Paul and I decided. Instead of following Paul's dream of starting his PhD program at the University of Iowa, we would move to Oklahoma City so that Carol and Chris could be close to our surrogate parents, Aunt Lorene and Uncle Leon. We prayed. I knew I needed help with Carol and Chris. By then, I was 22, Carol, 15, and Chris was 11. I felt there was enough age difference that I could be a good parent to Chris, but I wasn't sure about Carol. She was a full-fledged teenager – with all the potential of risk-taking in the near future. I would need some guiding wisdom from my aunt and uncle during my siblings' teenage years.

With a $10 roll of quarters, Paul and I drove to a pay phone to call Aunt Lorene. I remember the quarters dinging as they dropped into the pay phone. When Aunt Lorene answered, I began to explain our plan: Paul and I would move to Oklahoma City, I would get a teaching job, and the children would live with us. We just needed some support from them. Could we count on them?

My aunt, a strong-willed woman, interrupted to tell me she and Leon had decided to take the children into their home.

Lorene & Leon Crosswhite (surrogate parents), Carol and Chris

"No," I said, "you can't do that. I won't let you. Your children are married and gone from home; now is your time to enjoy life. Besides, you have a 2-bedroom home, so it's not big enough for them."

"Oh, yes, we can. We are selling our home and buying a 4-bedroom house. We've already looked at one and are ready to buy."

"No, you cannot do that. You don't know what you are doing. I've got this all figured out."

"Yes, Beverly, we do know what we are doing. You are too young. You are just starting your life. We can give them a good home."

"No, Aunt Lorene. I know I'm young, but I have taken care of them most of my life. Please listen to me. They are my responsibility, and I want to do this. I love them and they are mine."

"No, Beverly, that is not a good idea. You would have to have some help."

"OK, what about this, Carol can live with you and Chris can live with me and we will be close by and they can grow up together?"

"No, they need to stay together. Trust me, Beverly. Leon and I know what we are doing."

The argument continued until my quarters were gone.

She was right, but it broke my heart to know I could not step in as the substitute mother for Carol and Chris. Paul and I decided that the only and best thing to do was to move to Oklahoma City. We would help support the children with family activities until they reached adulthood. God would take care of us and our future. We need not fear.

Thankfully, Carol, Chris, and Ken spent the summer of 1970 with Dad's family in California. At summer's end, Carol and Chris returned from California and moved directly into a new house with Aunt Lorene and Uncle Leon. They never got to say goodbye to their stepfather and his wife; they had already moved away. Paul and I moved into my mother's home in Oklahoma City, which was still in her name. We set up house—just in time for my new job teaching special education. I had started a Master's degree in Learning Disabilities, but I wasn't certified yet. But no one else was either. I would figure it out as I went along. I had learned to trust my inner compass and my Soul Companion.

Chapter 6

Let the Children Come

My college diploma gave me a marketable degree. That had been my goal since my dad died. Now I was a full-fledged certified teacher. And I was excited about stepping into a classroom of my own. However, I had no idea what lay ahead. While every generation of teachers faces special challenges, mine had to grapple with one of historic dimensions: desegregation. I entered the stormy seas of social prejudices and racial warfare as well as adolescent immaturities as a first-year teacher in a public school of seventh, eighth and ninth graders. Immediately, I faced and learned to survive many kinds of clashes.

Up the Down Staircase

It was 1970, the first year of integration in the Oklahoma City Public School district. The all-white Eisenhower Junior High became 40% black overnight. The African-American students had been bussed from another part of town into Eisenhower. It was a tough first year.

Our country had just come through a brutal decade over the issue of integration. I knew racial discrimination must end if we were to survive as a nation. But, I had witnessed the assassinations of some promising young leaders—President John F. Kennedy, his brother Bobby, Martin Luther King, Jr. and others—who worked for a brighter future for *all* Americans, regardless of skin color or social status. With each death of our American heroes, my hope for racial harmony dwindled. Why did our country keep dragging the legacy of the Civil War from decade to decade?

A movie, "Up the Down Staircase," that had come out a couple years earlier, told a story of school integration from the eyes of a young and naïve teacher. On one of her first days as a teacher, not realizing the school had one-way staircases, up and down, she walked up the wrong one. An administrator on his way down, barked, "You're going up the down staircase!" I saw that type of clash over and over in my school. I identified with that teacher who only wanted to make a positive but vital difference in the lives of her students. I, too, was fighting an uphill battle to instill affirmative values in my students.

Looking back, it was a delicate, perilous, but yet an opportune time to be able to teach and influence young lives in the middle of desegregation. I soon realized that I was battling the segregation issue, and more. I was also struggling against the onerous structures and conditions of adolescents in what was increasingly called "K-12" education. The classes were overcrowded. I had 40 junior-high students in my eighth grade English class and 20 junior-high students in special education classes (today, special education classes are capped at 8-10). I wore my 4-inch heels and my just-above-the-knee dresses to look mature and respectable. How did my students know I was barely 22 and fresh out of school with only one semester of teaching experience? How could they not know? Once, I tried to break up a fight in the hallway and got in the middle of swinging fists. My colleagues, much older and wiser, told me not to break up the fights. "Go get the administration" they told me. Great! By the time I got to the principal's office, more fights had broken out. Sadly, the racial storms I encountered in that first year of teaching have raged on throughout my entire lifetime.

I taught special education classes for the "Educable Mentally Retarded" at Eisenhower. Although later renamed "Mildly Intellectually Disabled," at the time that particular special education program bore that ghastly name. My students were called "retards" by the other students. It pained me to see how they were so segregated from the other students. I thought this was the year for "integration." But integration of special needs children into the mainstream of education would not come for several more years. I know; I worked to bring that change for more than three decades.

Rodney, one of my special education students, won a special place in my heart. He was a six-foot-tall African American boy who towered over most of the teachers. He had been held back a couple of times, so he was already old enough to drive when he was in ninth grade. But, he wasn't a fighter, thank God. The main problem with Rodney was that he could not keep his upper jaw and lower jaw together. They were in constant motion. He made it almost impossible to teach the class about Einstein's Laws of Motion because of his incessant talking. The truth is, I really liked him and he knew it. One day Rodney, seeing my exasperation, said, "Miss Oxley, why don't you just tape my mouth shut with duct tape? That's what my other teachers do."

I looked at him in disbelief. Of course, I didn't believe him. That could be grounds for dismissal for a teacher. But, he was serious. In my desperation, I handed Rodney a roll of masking tape and told him to "have at it … I won't tape it, but you can if you want to." Rodney warned me that masking tape was not a good as duct tape and that it probably couldn't hold his mouth together very good. But, that's all I had. He sat at the back of the class as quiet as a fallen tree in winter. I taught a whole class without interference. But, then, lunch time came and the tape had to come off. He seemed very proud of himself for not interrupting my class. I never had the heart to use masking tape again. I just adapted to Rodney's ramblings. I guess he had to adapt to my ramblings, too. We understood each other.

One day I drove home across Oklahoma City in tears. I was in Paul's green '52 Plymouth. He needed our more dependable '65 Pontiac for the longer commute to the University of Oklahoma in Norman where he was working on a Master's degree in philosophy. That Plymouth was a thorn in my flesh, but good for my humility. Stick shift, no power steering, lights that turned off at will, and brakes that had to be pumped in order to stop the thing. The car even smelled old. Well, it was old! The closer I got home, the louder I was wailing. Could I stand another day of teaching junior-high kids amid the stress of desegregation? Was the teaching profession for me? Paul and I needed my salary to survive, but was teaching worth it?

As I reached home and drove into my driveway, I began to get a glimpse of why I was willing to endure a 25-mile drive across Oklahoma City to a school in turmoil. I had grown to love teaching because of the connections I made with students. I wanted a better life for them. My life was miserable only eight hours a day, but so many of theirs were in chaos 24 hours a day. I realized I needed to put on my big girl pants and rise to the challenge. I continued work on my Master's degree at a university 20 miles north of our home.

Looking back, I recognize that I needed that excruciating experience with junior high kids in the middle of desegregation to toughen me up for what I would encounter when I opened a counseling center 40 years later. That first year of teaching was my most challenging teaching experience ever, but I learned so much from it that I wouldn't trade it for a new Lexus. I learned that I loved kids, no matter their race, intellectual ability, social level, or age. But, I was also happy when a surprise call came to me the summer after that first year of teaching.

The Director of Special Education of the Putnam City Schools, where I lived, invited me to come by her office. In the interview she told me of a new Learning Disabilities program which Putnam City Schools would launch that fall. After hearing I was about to complete my Master's degree in LD, she offered me a job at Hefner Junior High, under Norman Dillard.

I would have an average of three to five students per class. My budget for materials was large. And Hefner was only seven miles from home. What's to decide with that kind of offer?

It was an exciting time to be teaching in the field of special education. Laws were being passed to ensure that all children—no matter how handicapped—could receive a free public education. Children with special needs had always touched my heart, so when I had the chance to teach them, I began to understand why I entered education.

Paul and I had our lives planned out—which included children in about five years. But, in our third year of marriage, I found out I was pregnant. I was not happy! We were both still going to grad school and barely scraping by. Eating lots of beans and cornbread because teachers' salaries in Oklahoma in those days were low – both in public schools and at Southwestern College where Paul was teaching. But my dismay about the pregnancy soon turned to acceptance and then to sheer elation.

Life, Altered

I was due in the middle of June. Perfect! I could teach through the end of the school year and resume the next fall. We decided to keep the news to ourselves for a while.

When I told Mr. Dillard, he looked somber. "Good news for you; bad for us." I assured him I could teach through the end of the school year.

"No, ma'am. You can't. We have a school policy that as soon as you start showing, you must take a maternity leave."

I was in shock. "Showing?" Was my forehead marked with the letter 'A?' Must I leave my job in disgrace? Seriously, I was a married woman, not a single one!

"That's the policy here, Mrs. Oxley. We'll find you a substitute as soon as you need it."

Fortunately for me, "tent" dresses were in style. So, everyone was wearing "maternity dresses." Because I was tall and thin, I carried my baby well until the seventh month. No one suspected anything, and I had enough sick leave to take off the last two months of school without losing pay.

Julinna Christine arrived on June 17, 1973. I had no idea motherhood would change me so radically. Julinna captured my heart the first time we gazed into each other's eyes. But she *really* stole her daddy's heart. We soon came to see how very bright and talented she was. When she was 2 years old, she walked through the house saying the word, "onomatopoeia." Paul and I looked at each other; we realized we better be careful with our conversation. The little parrot might repeat our words to her babysitter or strangers on the street. At age 3, she was reciting the Apostle's Creed. At age 6, she gave her first piano recital.

But, it was Julinna's profound empathy for others that caught me off guard. When she was just a toddler, she would see a child in distress, and look at me with a concerned furrowed brow. She wanted me to "fix" the problem for the child. (Later, Julinna wrote her PhD philosophy dissertation on the moral dimensions of empathy, using ethical theory as her basis.) For the first time in my life, I considered not going back to work after her birth so I could stay home and be a full-time mother.

But, our financial state dictated that I return to Hefner the following fall for another year of teaching. God answered our prayers for a caregiver for Julinna when I went back to work. She lived right around the corner. Ida Whaley, "Mimi" as Julinna would come to call her, was 50 years and 1 day older than Julinna and was a stay-at-home housewife. She and "Pa" had reared three bright and successful children. They had an empty nest. At first, Ida was hesitant to take on the responsibility of full-time childcare. But, as soon as I laid that winsome 2-month-old baby in Mimi's arms, they bonded with each other and became fast friends for years before Julinna started kindergarten. In fact, they were friends until Mimi's death more than 40 years later.

Mr. Dillard and the Special Education Director had a big discussion over my transfer to another school. In the end they let me decide, but it was clear that the Director had a few promotions in mind for me. The first one would be moving to Putnam City High School. In the fall of 1976, I did so reluctantly.

During the late '60s and '70s, illegal drugs had infiltrated the public schools and changed the educational achievement, the behavior, and even the atmosphere of the schools. Like most of the other schools in the area, drugs were a major problem at Putnam City High School, one of the top academic schools in Oklahoma. In one school day, seven students overdosed and were rushed to the hospital. I discovered that many of my special education students used illegal substances. How could that happen?

Fortunately, I became pregnant again that year and I decided not to return to the high school. By then, I was working on another degree in school psychology. My Director wanted me to come back to work as a school psychologist as soon as I returned from maternity leave. Rules had changed by that time; I could stay as long as possible until the baby came, even though I was "showing." Andeena was due the first of June, so I planned to teach until I could no longer waddle into class.

One of my special education students tried to help me go into labor early. As I sat at my desk, he came up behind me and dangled a live white mouse about two inches from my nose. I jumped high in the air while my swivel chair went sailing across the room. The teachers next door came running to see what the blood-curdling scream was all about. I'm sure it was a hilarious sight for all my students to see their very pregnant teacher leaning over her desk, about to pass out. The classroom was deathly silent; no one admitted who had done the dastardly deed, and the white mouse mysteriously disappeared. That's when I decided it was time to take my maternity leave. My heart could not take any more pranks like that one.

Andeena Kristeen arrived on May 25, 1977. Julinna was beside herself when we brought her little baby sister home. She had been kissing my tummy for months and just wanted to hold that little baby. It was love at first sight for her. Four years older, she thought she was big enough to be Andeena's nursemaid.

Andeena had a different temperament and skill set than Julinna's, but she was just as winsome and bright. She loved playing tricks on people, especially on holidays, so her unexpected pranks brought an air of joyful anticipation to special days. She also loved animals from the moment she saw one. By the time she was 2, she was begging for a "goggy." Even though I didn't share her love of animals, I couldn't resist the pleadings of that little girl whose eyes lit up when she saw dogs and cats. We got our first doggy when she was 2 and have had numerous pets since then – most of them rescued from death row.

Over the next five years, I was given opportunities to attend various trainings and seminars in the field of special education in Oklahoma and out-of-state to specialize in assessments of various disabilities: the blind, the deaf, the autistic, the multiple-handicapped. My job was also to serve as the "Child Find" coordinator in the Putnam City School system, which meant I sought out and publicized that *all* handicapped children could receive free appropriate public education beginning at birth up to age 21.

Until the "Education for All Children" laws were passed in 1975, children had to be toilet trained and "educable" in order to enter public schools. If they were deemed to be uneducable, they stayed home. So, after the passage of Public Law 94-142 in 1975, *all* children began attending public schools. It brought shockwaves to many school-aged children, school personnel, and to the public at large. My job placed me on the cutting edge of that major legislation, and I loved it. It was exciting to see these special needs children educated to their potential for the first time in American public school history.

Another significant change took place in my life over these first years of marriage. As mentioned previously, I had grown up with strong belief in the presence of God within us. During that time, I served our local church as Sunday School teacher for preschoolers as well as Children's Ministry Director. As such, I had responsibilities throughout the entire Sunday morning service. That rigorous schedule did not allow me to attend any Sunday morning church services. So, Paul and I took advantage of that opportunity to visit other churches in our area that held services at 8:00 a.m. We began to see the Body of Christ as a much larger ecumenical movement than that of our small denomination. We were exposed to the worship of Episcopals, Anglicans, Lutherans, Baptists, Methodists, Charismatic Catholics, and others. My hungry spirit would lead me to reading Mother Teresa, Dietrich Bonhoeffer, C.S. Lewis, and many other spiritual formation leaders.

I felt no inclination to leave the denomination of my childhood, but I grew spiritually through the rich teachings of those other Christian voices. After a few years in one local church, we moved our membership to the Yukon IPHC (International Pentecostal Holiness Church) church where Glynn and Michelle Bachelor were pastors. They immediately welcomed us into their heart and home and invited me to take leadership as Christian Education Director.

The Bachelors gave me the green light, and the people of the church followed like eager sheep heading toward green pastures. We implemented many novel and creative programs as the church grew. We built a "Noah's Ark" center for preschoolers. The Ark had a three-foot doorway cut in order to enter the classroom. The children loved it as they were able to walk into the classroom but their teachers had to crawl into the boat. (We did have another entrance for those unable to "become as little children in order to enter the Kingdom of Heaven.") Our teen center was a colorful blend of bright bold colors and cool seating. Outreach to the community was our pastor's vision, and he worked hard to take the gospel to those in need, whether they ever came to church or not. I had no idea that I would be leaving that thriving ministry during the height of growing success. But a wind began blowing that would change the direction of my life.

Georgia On My Mind

Paul, committed to his teaching position at Southwestern College of Christian Ministries in Oklahoma City, was not looking for another teaching position. But in early 1982 faculty friends at Emmanuel College encouraged him to apply for a teaching position opening up in the School of Christian Ministries. When he asked me to begin praying about moving to Georgia, I was surprised. I had only been east of the Mississippi River once. How could we leave the life we had built in Oklahoma City and move to a foreign land? Perhaps at least we should visit the campus before we decided.

And we did. We flew to Atlanta, rented a car, and drove through Atlanta traffic without proper knowledge of where to exit. God surely assigned four guardian angels around our vehicle to protect other drivers from us. There was no GPS in those days and the printed map we had did not show Franklin Springs – only Royston. It was truly an uncharted town. We had been given directions but they were difficult to follow in the dark. As we exited the interstate and got on country roads, I saw cows grazing in the fields beside the road, and we caught sight of old falling down shacks, among newer homes. With each passing mile of the 13 miles of country road, my heart sank deeper and deeper. I felt certain God was tricking us. He was just testing us to see if we would be willing to go to the far side of the desert. As soon as we convinced Him we would, He would say, "Good job, Paul and Bev. You passed the test. Now, you can return to Oklahoma City."

We finally arrived at our hosts' home around 11:00 that night. We had planned to be there several hours earlier but we could not notify them of our delay without phones available. The lovely couple, Earl and Nancy Beatty, greeted us warmly at the door. Soon, we were sitting around their kitchen table with warm stew and other snacks they had prepared. We could not have felt more welcomed.

The next day we went to their favorite watering hole – the Roystonian. We had ham and eggs and something called "grits." I had heard of grits, but had never eaten them. After taking a bite, I swallowed lots of orange juice to wash them down. But, the biscuits made up for the tasteless grits. Big and buttery and served with gravy on the side. This place could easily put weight on you.

Franklin Springs had a population of less than 1,000, one red light, and not one fast-food restaurant! The larger and nearby Royston was the real "city," with a population of 3,500. Total population of this geographical area was about the same as the high school enrollment where I taught one year. How on earth could we survive without our family, friends, and life we had built together for 12 years in Oklahoma City?

After a few days of interviews, looking around at homes, and meeting some of the friendliest people I'd ever met, Paul and I flew back home. We faced a big decision.

Three months later we were packing. The longest time I could imagine being away from my family in Oklahoma was two years. For Paul, the move carried no conditional time frame, but it was just as painful. When he told his parents who lived in Kansas of our move to Georgia, his mother cried. "You might as well be moving to Africa because I won't ever get to see my grandbabies." Sadly, she got to see them only two or three times before she died in a car accident in 1985.

As we packed up the possessions we had collected in 12 years, my mind drifted to the life we had built in Oklahoma City and the reasons we had moved there in the first place. My sister Carol was married and had a beautiful daughter. My brother Chris had graduated with his degree in pre-med and had been accepted into medical school. He had been married for one year. So, my precious living cargo of a younger brother and sister had been delivered to their destination. Aunt Lorene and Uncle Leon had taken most of the responsibility for their successful entry into adulthood. I had simply supported them, but I, too, felt I had fulfilled my responsibility. Carol and Chris simply didn't need me as much any longer, so I was free to move on.

At 9 years old, Julinna entered fourth grade in Georgia. She had begun piano lessons at age 6 and was progressing rapidly. I hoped we could find the same kind of patient and encouraging piano teacher in

Georgia. We did—Carol White, a gifted musician with a full slate of piano students.

Andeena was very bright, but didn't seem to share her sister's love for school. She would much rather play and have a good time. She entered kindergarten in Georgia. I prayed for an easy transition for all of us. After all, in my mind it was for only two years in this small rural town and then we could resume our lives in civilization.

I looked at our home we were leaving in Oklahoma. It was the second home we had resurrected from the dead and brought to new life. It was beautiful. I remembered how Paul had worked so hard to make it a comfortable home. His most challenging project was wallpapering the 24-foot walls in the entry and living room. With an impressive cathedral ceiling and sky-light windows, it was an Architectural Digest show home plopped down in the middle of Oklahoma City. We had grown to love that unique home. Because of his fear of heights, I stood at the bottom of the scaffolding, holding it steady for him to hang the wallpaper while encouraging him to "look up, honey, not down."

It's interesting how we become attached to the things we invest a lot of time in. For a woman, a home represents a haven of peace and security. It seemed I was cashing all that in for a pot of porridge. I would have to start all over in our Georgia home because it needed a lot of work to be resurrected from the dead.

I was also leaving a job I loved. I had helped to establish a Learning Disabilities program at a junior high and high school. I had also been highly trained in assessments of all 12 categories of special needs children, and I had mentored many new teachers and assessors in the field. I had two babies and did not miss a beat with work. Life had been good in this place.

And our church family had become family over our years at the Yukon church. We all cried at the farewell service on Sunday before we left town on Monday morning.

Our friends and family asked why we were leaving all that we had built there. It made no sense to them. Didn't make such sense to me either. Or the kids. All we knew was that we had felt a call deep in our spirits to go to the other side of the desert, to Franklin Springs. And we were going – even though we faced many changes and, perhaps, troubled waters ahead. I had no idea at the time how this move to Georgia would change my entire future.

Chapter 7

Desert Storms

Like all moves, I suppose, our relocation from Oklahoma to Georgia followed a common life pattern. We gather up all our baggage, our stuff, and roll it down the road to new places. And we assume things will be different in a new house, new job, new church, new stores and restaurants, and in the other new details of life. But, in time, we see nothing changed.

We also brought ourselves and our old bundles of weaknesses, strengths, fears, joys, guilts, and futilities. As we unpack our possessions, we also unpack all that. Before long, all the same old psycho rivers flow through and around and over us. With such a move, it's possible that we become estranged from our church, community, family, and even ourselves.

The mental health disorder called "clinical depression" can be the outcome of this estrangement. Little did I know when we first arrived in Georgia that I was about to enter the greatest storm of my life.

But, I've also discovered that every move also brings real change. As I look back now, I know some of our baggage fell away in Oklahoma. God visited our places in the heart. Like the great Exodus of God's people from Egypt back to the land of promise, our move to Franklin Springs, Georgia took us away from some oppressive burdens into the

Lord's more generous provision for us. Looking back, it was only after I had been overtaken by depression and recovered from it that I was able to see this.

We almost didn't make it out of Oklahoma City. Paul drove a 24-foot Ryder truck and I drove a 15-foot U-Haul pulling Paul's 1970 Volkswagen Karmann Ghia, his vintage pride and joy. When I changed lanes on the interstate about five miles from our home, I heard screeching tires and blaring horns. The next thing I saw was an unlovely hand gesture from a driver I had almost run off the road.

The rest of the thousand-mile, four-day journey carried additional episodes of a tire blow-out, broken headlights, sick children and two exhausted drivers (Mommy and Daddy), among other human dramas. And, just like our spiritual ancestors, the Children of Israel, God used our long journey to purge some habits and attitudes that would not be suitable in the new land.

When we finally drove up to our rented house in Franklin Springs, I turned the U-Haul truck into a driveway as steep as a ski slope, burying the hitch of the trailer deep into the asphalt. So, we had to unload the truck from the street, carrying everything up that long ski slope. Paul's truck fared even worse, getting bogged down in the front yard mud with an even longer distance to carry heavy furniture. With new friends to help us, we had a perfect ending to our four-day saga of adversity. We were finally unpacked into our new home. On the back side of what was to become to me – 'the desert.'

I don't know what I was thinking when I told the local Special Education Director that I would teach the Deaf and Hearing-Impaired classes that 1982-83 school term. Good grief! I only had a couple of classes in sign language; I certainly wasn't proficient in it. But the certified teacher of the deaf was on maternity leave and they had *no one* to teach this handful of students. I'm sure administration conversations probably ran something like this: "Hey, nobody in their right mind would do it, but ask Mrs. Oxley; she'll do anything!"

So, there I was with five students, four of them totally deaf. Only one hearing impaired. That meant I *had* to know American Sign Language (ASL) in order to communicate with them – *at all.* I was also expected to *teach* them something. One was in elementary, three in middle school, and one in high school. I later learned that a national outbreak of rubella during a three-four-year period in the late 1960s had caused deafness in utero for thousands of babies. I worked with five of them every day.

When classes began, I tried my best to introduce myself by spelling out my name in fingerspelling. "My name is … M…R…S… ……O…X…L…E…Y." They finally understood. Then they pointed to the chalkboard. What? What about it? Slowly, I realized they were telling me, "Just write it on the board." Duh!

"Oh. Yes. OK," I mumbled. They were deaf, not blind, I reminded myself.

Those kids were the kindest, most patient students I ever taught. I loved those kids! They taught me so much that year. I should have shared my salary with them; they were the real teachers. After a while, they gave up on using ASL with me and just started using hand and body motions and sound effects that I could understand. It was hysterical! But they really wanted to teach me, and I really wanted to teach them something. We actually learned a lot together that year and we all stayed in contact for many years.

Desert Storms

By the spring of our first year in Georgia, depression began to overtake me like a slow Georgia rain that went on and on without relenting, soaking the ground deeper and deeper. Within a few months I began to feel like I was trapped in a place I couldn't escape. I had left behind my family, friends, a stimulating job in a high-ranking school system, our lovely home we spent five years restoring, and our church where I had served as Christian Education Director. I felt I had traded in a Ferrari for a broken-down, rusted-out Volkswagen bus. My life in Oklahoma had been rich in social relationships with family and friends and in spiritual devotion. Now here I was in Franklin Springs, a God-forsaken place to me.

As a psychologist, I understand how our inability to cope with change can open up attacks from the enemy of our soul. When we feel unwanted, unneeded, or outright rejected, it can feel like life is not worth living. I never felt that way in Oklahoma so why did I feel that way now? It felt contradictory, both personally and emotionally.

To illustrate the incongruity of my life, people in Georgia kept asking me, "Where are you from?" When I told them "Oklahoma," they asked if I were a Yankee.

"No. Oklahoma was a neutral Indian territory during the Civil War, so we did not take any side." So whose side was I on now? This came to be not just a question of North/South geography or culture, but personal identity. Depression with the feeling of 'lostness' from God has a way of getting you to lead a double life– the exterior one we show others and the interior one known only to self. I was living on both sides.

On the exterior I was jovial and fun-loving. Paul and the girls seemed to be adjusting well to the new place. Paul was immersed in teaching Bible and theology at Emmanuel College. Julinna and Andeena had made friends and liked their new school. The pastor of the church was one of the finest. Whether or not I wanted to admit it, I came to see that many Southerners were some of the most generous folk around. One clothing store owner I barely knew offered to lend me her own personal red blouse for a special occasion because she didn't have one in her store for sale. And, a furniture store owner delivered new furniture to our home and told us "just pay for it whenever you can... no interest!" I was dumbfounded.

On the interior I was desperately unhappy and wanted to distance myself from Southerners. In what may be the legacy of the Civil War (what many of them call "the war of northern aggression"), they seem to bear a reproach, which makes them appear defensive. One colleague commented, "You foreigners come here, suck up our water, criticize our way of speaking, and insist we change our ways of doing things." Now, I admit I may have provoked that response when I commented about "Georgia not being very progressive." I learned really soon that "progress" was a bad word to some people in our neck of the woods in rural northeast Georgia.

Despite what appeared to be the good life on the outside, the incongruity of living a double life got the best of me. I was deeply hurt by certain church people who opposed me as being their Christian Education Director, so I resigned. I began to drift and felt like I was sinking into quicksand in this desert place. I was thinking and doing things – or not doing things that only a depression and lostness from God can cause. I felt forsaken by God. What was happening to me? Was I going through some kind of midlife crisis? Was I in genetic bondage to my Dad's dreams of having material "stuff" and success? I wanted out of that desert place before I died in it.

The Soul in a Dark Night

My depression continued to deepen. During the worst of it, I felt utterly abandoned by God. I questioned my faith. During these months of soul-searching and tears, I began to understand some of the purpose for my depression. My relationship with God had been broken. My childhood faith was important to stabilize me through the storms of my early life, but now that faith was not strong enough to take me where God wanted to lead. I had to go through the fire to rid more dross from my life.

I began to understand that Jesus Himself felt abandoned by His Father when He was stretched out on the cross. Jesus' pain was so excruciating that God seemingly turned His back on His Son because it was too much for the Father to bear. For a moment in time, Jesus cried out in agony, "My God, My God, why have you forsaken me?" Perhaps the greatest heartbreak possible: He would die alone.

Some years later, during a time of spiritual hunger and restlessness, I read several books by ancient church fathers and mothers (John of the Cross, St. Teresa of Avila, St. Francis of Assisi, etc.) who had experienced a "dark night of the soul." Looking back, I now can see that depression can have a spiritual purpose. It can make us or break us. It can draw us nearer to God or drive us far from Him. It's our choice to make, not His. If we relentlessly press into Him, even though we feel nothing, we can come out on the other side with an unshakeable faith. That is what happened to me. The storm did not drown me, it perfected me.

Out of God's incomprehensible mercy and love, He was not willing that I perish. Even though I felt abandoned by Him, He was ever so near me. He sent two Southern ladies into my life to rescue me. Barbara James invited me to attend a Bible study in her home. The moment I walked into her home, I felt safe and accepted. I was no longer an outsider. She was an anointed teacher and her home was packed out with other women eager to learn about God and the Bible, and who also wanted friendships. That safe and warm environment pointed me to the lighthouse away from the churning waters of depression.

Then God sent another Southern lady as a personal guide to help me. Carolyn Moore, a painfully honest and discerning new friend, led me through the murky and turbulent waters of my depression. Her words came out salty; no sugar coating. At first, I was intimidated by her. But I soon realized that God sent her to help me out of that horrible funk.

Carolyn and I taught in the same high school. She was a math teacher, and she carried great influence throughout the school. She was one teacher that students didn't dare cross. Once, a student walked up behind the school principal and smacked him on the back of the head and then quickly dodged into the boys' bathroom before the principal saw him.

But eagle-eyed Carolyn saw the whole thing. She marched into that bathroom and told that young man, "Get out of here right now!" She then jerked him in front of the principal. "Now, do to his face what you did to his back!"

God knew I needed that kind of friend. I was a lost puppy trying to find a home. I had tried to be accepted by the church and the community, but I just didn't fit the culture. I felt rejected. I felt I could not measure up to God's standards. I had no sense of purpose. The ropes that had tied me to the mast had weakened. I kept thinking about death; I wanted to take a slow walk out of that community and never go back. I felt I was perishing in this desert place.

But God wouldn't let me leave. He had plans for me, plans that would have terrified me if He had told me about them. All He told me was that He understood how I felt and that He would help me through it. I just needed to trust Him that I could be restored. But trusting Him also meant trusting Carolyn as a spiritual guide. I knew if I didn't accept His help, I would self-destruct. I was that depressed. I was that deep in despair.

Dancing in the Desert

Then, on a weekend in November 1984, in a musical concert at Emmanuel College and in the Franklin Springs church, God used Ken Medema to help me out of my pit of despair. Ken was (and, of this writing, still is) a uniquely gifted composer, often creating songs on the spot. He is also blind, but that gentleman can see things that others can't! As soon as he began composing an extemporaneous song called "Dancing in the Desert," I knew it held the secret to my being rescued from the encompassing waves of depression. Tears streamed down my face as his words bathed my heart:

I never will forget, never will forget, the day I started dancing in the desert.
It was a very strange thing, a very strange thing, the way this experience occurred to me.
I was dancing down the main road, with all my friends beside me... dancing down the main road, with everyone to guide me. All the lovely images of home ... to my heart's content.

When all at once He came along, and said:
"I want you to dance on the desert sand."
I asked him "why?" – it seemed so strange to me.
He said, ***"There are lessons only the desert can teach you.***
Time for you to learn; it's time for you to be growing up.
Unless you go to the desert, I just can't reach you.

You need comforts taken away from you.
You've got good friends and a good home, the children...."

So I turned off the road and went into the desert and there I danced on the desert sand until I dropped. I was thirsty and hungry and I said, "Lord, will you take care of me?"
And He was silent. Not a word did he say; not a sound did He make.

I ran and walked and shouted and screamed, "Please don't let me die. Please take care of me. Please! You can't imagine how it feels to be alone in the desert."
All at once I saw a desert cactus. I saw the plant growing there.
"Must be very hard to grow," I said. "How do you live in this desert sand, cactus?"

"I learn to live simply and I learn not to demand too much; I take nothing for granted, I learn to be frugal. Maybe you should learn it too."

I heard His voice saying, ***"Now go back to the road …now go back to the highway. You have learned the cactus lesson … may you never forget the lessons."***

You don't need a whole lot of stuff.
… You need the Lord of the dance.

Dancing can be simple.
You don't need a brand new car.
You don't need new houses. …
You don't need a lot of expensive trappings.
They can get you in a hell of a lot of trouble.
You don't need them.

You need the Lord of the Desert and the lesson of the desert cactus and His wings beneath your feet.
One of these days you'll be dancing on the universal dance floor and your dancing will be complete."[4]

There it was—the foundation of my life in Oklahoma City had been my success as a teacher, as a school psychologist, as a Christian Education Director. It had all been propped up by my overweening pride—the beautiful home in a lovely neighborhood, my high-ranking job, respect from family and friends and colleagues. And we had been surrounded by our vast family. People who loved us and provided a sense of security and stability. When all those external props were taken away, I fell deeply into depression. Pride almost took my life. Indeed, "Pride goeth before destruction and a haughty spirit before a fall." (Prov. 16:18, KJV) I had memorized that verse as a child, but I experienced its truth as a middle-aged adult.

Medema's song opened my eyes to see I didn't need all the trappings of worldly success or possessions or even a family nearby. In fact, just as he sang, those things "can get you into a hell of a lot of trouble." Yep, I had known that hell for more than two years.

And I heard His clear word: Live simply and frugally. Look not to "stuff" or "success," but look to the Lord of the Desert who will teach you to dance wherever He places you—in plenty or in want, in prison or in open spaces, with princes or with paupers, with or without family. The dance of freedom is *within* us, not *outside* us. I did not know I would one day dance jubilantly on the desert floor.

In time, fresh breezes moved the desert storms away. Eventually, daylight and green grass, flowers and rainbows and reality reappeared.

4 Used by permission, Ken Medema Music, www.kenmedema.com.

The joy of living returned. My life's purpose would never have been revealed without time in the desert. After showing me the beauty and power of arid places, He didn't release me to return to my well-watered world. No, He called me deeper into the sweeping expanse of more desert places he had prepared for me.

Kenya

Over the years Paul's heart had been turning more and more toward missions in various ways – financially supporting several missionaries, being the faculty sponsor of the John F. Freeman Missions Club at Emmanuel, and serving as Missions Director of our local church. In the summer of 1986 he was invited to be the first teacher at the Eldoret Bible Training Center in western Kenya. When he returned from that summer of teaching, I knew he had formed meaningful, permanent relationships with the staff and students at the school.

So, in January of 1989, I shouldn't have been caught off guard when he said to me, "Are you ready to move to Africa for a year?" He said that I, too, could teach and fill in for a missionary who was coming to the States on furlough.

At first, I thought it was a preposterous idea. Leave our home, our jobs, our friends, and our church? Hadn't we already taken that test? What? Did we not pass it? Was God asking us to do it again? Did He ask Abraham to kill Isaac a second time? Was He seriously asking us to leave Georgia and move to Kenya for a year? I was numb. I had only thought that rural Georgia was the back side of the desert. Kenya was truly and deeply on the back side of the desert. 10,000 miles away from civilization. Well, at least that far from *my* civilization.

Paul had been on several mission trips by that time, but I had never joined one. I had only been out of the USA one time—as a child, walking 50 yards into Mexico with my mom and dad. Did God not remember He hadn't called me to the foreign mission field?

But, when I calmed down and began to listen, I knew Paul felt called to short-term missions. I took a deep breath; maybe I should consider it for my husband's sake.

We would need to be in Kenya by June 1989. That meant we had exactly five months to raise our own support—about $50,000 for that year in Kenya. I would have to resign my job; Paul could take a leave of absence from Emmanuel. And, oh yes, it would be nice if the girls would be on board to leave their friends, school, church, and go to a strange place on the dark and often dangerous side of the desert. It seemed like an impossible, if not absurd, hare-brained thing to do. Raise $50,000 in five months? Live in someone else's home? They would live in our home? Quit my job? What would our children say?

We began to contact churches, friends, and family about financial support. My faith was not immense, but I did believe that God would provide for us if we said "yes" to this calling. But by March only a meager amount had been pledged toward our mission. Paul and I had both told our employers that next year we would not return to our jobs. Without the financial support how could we go? Paul and I had initially mapped out and contacted the churches and persons most likely to provide the financial support for our mission. But, for whatever reason, we did not get the response we thought we would.

On a Sunday afternoon in March, when we were about to call it quits, we got a call from a pastor in North Carolina who told us his church was wanting to support us $200 a month while in Kenya. We were speechless. Not only had we not contacted him about supporting us, but we hardly knew him. Soon other churches and people whom we had not initially contacted began to notify us of their support. We were learning that God's thoughts are higher than ours and His ways are better than ours. God is the ultimate source of our provision.

The fact of the matter is that our friends and our home church, the Franklin Springs Pentecostal Holiness Church, provided not only finances, but intangible support throughout our year away to let us know we were not alone. Our pastor, Dr. Doug Beacham and his wife Susan, were enthusiastic supporters. Not only did he lead the church in its financial support of our mission, he agreed to teach Paul's New Testament Greek class at Emmanuel College for the year Paul was on leave of absence.

So, these Southerners whom years ago I believed did not like us, were the heart of the support in our mission work. The year before, they had proven their love for me on my 40th birthday when, it seems, much of the community teased and played tricks on me to celebrate my "Lordy, Lordy, Beverly's Forty" birthday. And I played pranks on them right back. How I had grown to love these Southerners who genuinely and deeply loved and had fun together.

Paul was part of that unforgettable 40th birthday celebration. After encouraging me to "put on your white hose, heels, and nicest dress," he and the girls took me to dinner – not to my favorite fancy restaurant I had envisioned, but an outdoor hotdog stand! There the four of us sat on a concrete picnic table dressed in our best in the sweltering Georgia summer heat, as cars passed by staring at this strange sight. When word got around the community of his antics (which spread like wild-fire), Paul became a hero in the eyes of the men, but a villain in the eyes of the women—including mine! Thirty years later, people in the community still talk about Paul's bravery on my 40th birthday. I just roll my eyes.

On June 7, 1989 (one day before my 41st birthday), we flew out of the Atlanta airport bound for Kenya with sufficient money in our account to rent a house, pay utilities, eat, and have transportation for six months. We believed the rest would come in when needed. And it did. It was my second airplane ride and the first out of the United States. The kids had never flown before.

For my birthday celebration, we took a canal cruise in Amsterdam. I can't remember much about it because our heads were nodding through most of it (it was 2:00 in the morning for us). A pigeon did give me a small birthday present on the shoulder of my white sweater when Paul took inordinately long to take my picture. I was hollering at Paul to hurry up when the bird landed on my shoulder, but he was trying to get the camera settings just right. Like I've jokingly said a few dozen times, "If cameras are in heaven, I'm going to re-think the whole thing."

So many doors opened, one right after another. I kept a prayer journal. That series of provisions and clear words of direction strengthened our faith beyond anything we had experienced. For example, we prayed for Julinna to be admitted to Rift Valley Academy (RVA) in Kijabe, Kenya. The African Inland Mission (AIM) boarding school for missionary kids and nationals was considered one of the best schools on the African continent. RVA was about a four-hour drive from where we would be living in Eldoret. I knew it would be a good place for her to be educated that year, but they had a long waiting list. Without God's help, she would probably not get in for the fall term.

Soon after we arrived in Kenya, a missionary friend, David List, took Julinna and us to RVA for a visit. David, a former student and student body president of RVA, was well known to the administration. At the close of the visit, David told Julinna that RVA would admit her for that fall. Coincidental meeting? No. I believe God used it to fulfill His purposes.

That year in Kenya was the best of times and the worst of times for me. I loved living in Eldoret, a city of half a million people, close to the equator at 7,000 feet high. The climate was very hot in the

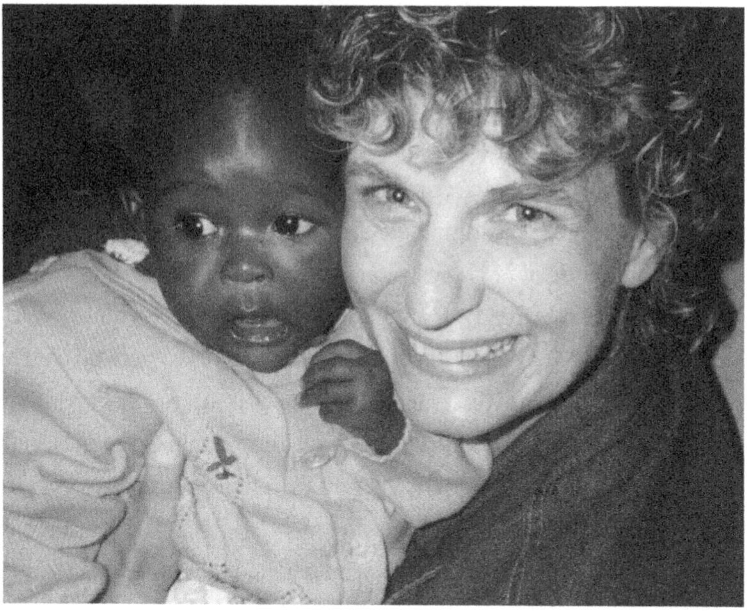

Beverly and Mercy (Kenyan friends)

direct sun, but cool in the shade. We slept in sweat suits most nights. We lived on a compound in a large house with a young man to help with household responsibilities and gardening. We boiled our milk and water, ate fresh fruits and vegetables, and, when we could get it, ate the best meats available. We made friends with most of the other missionaries—35-40 of them from England, Wales, Korea, Denmark, Australia, and America. We also built close friendships with many of our Kenyan brothers and sisters. Julinna remembers that year in Kenya as one of the best of her childhood.

At that time, Kenya had no special education in public schools. Not surprising because Kenya didn't even have compulsory education. And school attendance was fee-based.

Down the street from our home in Eldoret, John and Esther Greene presided over a private day school (preschool through high school). They had founded the school decades earlier. I soon learned they also had an orphanage on the campus for about a hundred children. The school fees helped support the orphanage.

When John came to Kenya from England on a one-way ticket, he stumbled into a ministry for street kids who were rummaging for food. From that fledging beginning, he established one of the most highly ranked schools in all of Kenya, along with an orphanage.

When John learned of my background in special education, he asked me to come help a few of the orphans who were struggling academically. He was concerned about their ability to support themselves if they did not get an education. That invitation led to me establishing a special education program at the orphanage, the first program of its kind in Eldoret.

After assessing their strengths and deficits, I developed individual education plans for each student. Not only did they catch up with other students, but they felt good about themselves, perhaps for the first time. And, many behavioral problems disappeared. Today, most of those kids are successfully employed, married, and have children.

Some of those children still ask to see me when I visit Eldoret. How gratifying to see them as responsible adults, contributing to the good of society.

Eldoret, Kenya is located on the main road about midway from Nairobi, Kenya to Kampala, Uganda. In that central location, we had many opportunities to show bed-and-breakfast hospitality to missionaries who needed overnight lodging. Soon after our arrival in Kenya, I had a most humiliating experience. Our East Africa mission leader was coming through our town with two other dignitaries en route to Uganda and asked for lodging. I invited them to dinner that evening. A catastrophe of immeasurable proportions was about to occur.

In that one meal alone, I learned many cooking lessons: Kenyan rice requires several sortings to remove all the tiny rocks, making Jell-O with fresh pineapple prevents congealing, and baking at 7,000 feet of altitude causes ingredients to overflow. When my guests chomped down on the rice dish I had carefully prepared, they started grabbing their jaws. Pain in the teeth! I finally realized what I had done and told them to stop eating the rice dish. I didn't have money to pay for all their dental bills! Then, as I proudly brought in the Jell-O made with fresh pineapple in my fancy individual stemmed bowls, it was so watery, it splashed onto the tablecloth and they had to drink it from the cups. I had also made a beautiful pecan pie with pecans I brought from Georgia. Because of the high altitude, the filling and pecans had boiled over onto the oven floor so all that was left was a piece of crust with a syrupy film on it.

I've never been known for my great culinary skills, but this dinner outdid them all. And I couldn't even hide my face after that disgusting dinner. Our guests spent the night and I had to feed them again the next morning. I'm sure they were reluctant to come to my breakfast table. Cereal and milk with fresh fruit. That was it. I didn't want to risk making toast. I had previous experience with my 110-volt kitchen appliances using 220 voltage via a transformer, which didn't always transform. No need to chance another debacle. We all, including our guests, breathed a communal sigh of relief when they left our home. If the story of my disastrous dinner spread far and wide among the missionaries, I never knew. No one ever brought it up to me, so I was able to experience my disgrace in privacy.

Many people who have lived in equatorial Africa have had malaria. In September, I, too, contracted a serious malarial infection. I ran a fever of 105 degrees for a few days and passed in and out of delirium. Finally, when Paul found a trustworthy doctor, I began to pull out of it.

I was never able to donate blood again to the Red Cross. When I tried, they spotted the malaria in my blood sample and refused it. I guess they didn't want to start an epidemic of malaria in the United States.

After we had been in Kenya about six months, I drove into downtown Eldoret, when I suddenly had an overwhelming sense of well-being. In that moment, I knew I would be all right if Paul wanted to do mission work full-time. That's when the worst of times became the best of times.

When I told Paul about my epiphany, he thanked me, but said he didn't believe God called him to be a full-time missionary. He saw his work and our life should remain in the US, but that he wanted to be available to take short-term teams to Africa and other places. I put that piece of information in my hopper and let it settle. I had no idea we would do just that over the next two decades.

Return to America

Our year in Kenya turned into 14 months. While the months seemed to drag in the beginning, they picked up speed when the time to return grew nearer. In some ways, we were the same people who left Georgia the previous year, but in other ways that year changed us forever. We had found a new faith in God. Every penny of our expenses came in. We lacked for nothing. No bills were ever late. We had sufficient money to get back home and pick up our former jobs. But nothing extra. It was just enough. Manna in the desert was sufficient provision for the day, nothing more. Yes, a job was waiting for me when I arrived from Kenya.

I'm sure Paul, Julinna, and Andeena could tell you what they learned about God and themselves during those 14 months. For me, I found continuing confidence to dance in the desert. More than that, I discovered the Lord of the Desert. Because of Him, I found the courage and grace to live simply and frugally. He taught me to look to Him, not things or "success." He taught me to flourish wherever He placed me, with whatever gifts He had given me—to bloom wherever I was planted.

I also found the audacity to travel outside my comfort zones, to drive in the left-hand lanes with a stick shift, and to flow with inefficiency and a bribe-based economy. I found the capacity to accompany others to unfamiliar places so that they, too, could broaden their worldview and appreciate God's variegated patterns of peoples and cultures around the globe. Over the next two decades, Paul and I became part of many teams around the globe.

Our adventure of leading mission teams began soon after our return. Over the next few years, we took six teams to East Africa. Remarkably, from each team we took to Africa, at least one person ended up as a full-time missionary. One team saw seven out of eight team members enter full-time mission work. Although I never felt called to mission work myself, I sensed my calling was to help introduce young people to international Christian work.

Today, I can see clearly the steady hand of my Soul Companion as He gently escorted me from a wounded and sheltered childhood into teaching me to thrive in any circumstance. He led me out of self-doubt, away from reliance on false props, and beyond fear, rejection, cynicism, and defensiveness.

In more recent years, He taught me to dance—even audaciously—through illness and pain and aging. But, even more than that, God pushed me beyond myself, beyond what I thought I could do or tolerate. Setting me free to dance in the desert was preparation for providing a higher kind of care for His children in a tiny place called Franklin Springs, tucked away in a remote corner of Georgia. He helped me unlock the fountain of His majestic touch for wounded children and adults. Just as He stooped to enter our earth space as a human 2,000 years ago, I watched Him bend down to lift those who could not rise. And I was given a front row seat to witness it.

Incongruities will always be a part of life. Life is messy, unpredictable, and often unjust. The blue skies of today may turn into blue moods tomorrow. Pandemics may come and go. But, when we trust our Soul Companion, blue skies seem to always return after the storm.

Chapter 8

Dancing in the Desert

In the spring of 1997, my life changed dramatically and permanently. It all started when, at 49 years old, I began thinking of returning to Georgia State University for a PhD in psychology.

That marathon of studies imposed several hurdles for me. Its location in downtown Atlanta, nearly 100 miles from my home, meant commuting a couple afternoons a week after work—a 200-mile round trip into one of the most congested cities in America—at rush hour. That meant twice a week I would drop exhausted into bed around midnight. Two days later, repeat. On weekends, every weekend, I would have to devote time to statistics, research design, and psychopharmacology. Then, repeat (although in different courses) every semester. Every summer. For as long as it took. I hoped it would be no more than three or four years.

I wasn't afraid of the traffic, and wasn't afraid of statistics. Loved math, so not a problem. Loved coursework. Loved writing. But the greatest challenge was that, at the end of this thing, if I completed the program, I would have to defend my dissertation. In front of my dissertation committee. That was a terrifying thought. My sixth grade experience of freezing up and taking a zero for a three-minute reading in front of the class was never far from my mind. Even at 49, my palms got sweaty just thinking about it.

The only reason I even considered the PhD project was I felt God leading me to do it. So I took the Graduate Record Exam (GRE) again as part of the admittance requirements. I figured that if I bombed out, I would automatically be disqualified. Then maybe God and my thoughts wouldn't hassle me anymore. But, soon, I got a letter of acceptance.

Unfinished Business

In the spring of 1997, I also enrolled in Gary Moon's Institute of Clinical Theology. The one-year, four-course program helped psychologists integrate theology and psychology. In addition to the academic requirements, we would meet for four days every three months in a Clinical Theology Institute at a retreat center in Atlanta.

In our second course of the Clinical Theology Institute, Dr. Siang-Yang Tan from Fuller Theological Seminary led a course in "lay counseling." As part of his training, he demonstrated various techniques, using volunteers from our group of 12. He had already used a couple volunteers and nothing bad or embarrassing happened to them. So when he asked for another volunteer, I stepped up. I thought I would be safe.

Dr. Tan brought me to the front of the class and sat me in a chair beside him. He didn't ask any warm-up questions. He just told me to close my eyes. As I relaxed, he asked, "If your dad walked into this room tonight, what would you say to him?" I had told him nothing except both my parents had died early in my life.

As I described in Chapter 3, when my dad died, I never grieved for him. I was too angry, hurt, and scared to face his death. But I had never been able to forgive him for the pain he caused Mom and me and maybe others I didn't know about. It wasn't that I hadn't tried to forgive him. I had rationally thought through it, spoke the words "I forgive you," and moved on. Didn't work. I cried until my eyes were puffy and red. I wrote him letters. Nice, respectful letters. Nasty, mean, cut-to-the-chase letters. None of those steps worked. I couldn't seem to get free from the chains that held me hostage. But, after all the years, I rarely thought of him anymore. I did not recognize any need to take care of any unfinished business. I had a life, so I buried it. Deep!

I had no idea that I was the one who needed to be forgiven.

After sitting with my eyes closed for quite a while, I finally answered Dr. Tan's question, "I wouldn't say anything to him. I would smack him in the face." I was shocked at my own words. The depth of my rage and resentment toward Dad had hardened me to the point of hatred. And I justified it by blaming him for making my life miserable, for abusing my mother, for the hypocrisy of hidden sins. But, hatred toward him was just as bad if not worse than his rejection of me.

All of us share certain weaknesses—cowardice in the face of injustice, bigotry, pride, timidity, crushing bruised reeds (Isaiah 42:3), and indifference to the conditions of the poor and abused. God was doing something deep in my spirit in that moment. He would not allow me to hide behind self-righteous judgment of my dad on the grounds of *his* sins when *my* sins flashed in neon lights.

Dr. Tan told me to keep my eyes closed and see if any images came to my mind. One popped up: "I am in the fifth grade and my dad happens to be home when my report card comes out. Because he travels so much and can be gone for months at a time, I hope he will see my report card and express some kind of approval for my straight A's. That is the best shot I have at getting a smile from him. Not my looks. Not charm. Not musical or artistic talent. Just academic skills. If he doesn't approve of that, I have no hope of ever feeling loved by him."

"Now, I see myself as a 10-year-old sticking my report card in front of my dad. I want him to see my report card. I want his praise, a pat on the head, any recognition at all. He pushes me away and says, 'I'll look at it later. Can't you see I'm busy now?'"

And, right there, the pain of that moment 39 years before came back full force. I doubled over in my chair like I had been kicked in the stomach by a horse. I bawled! People in the class kept handing me tissues. The floor around my chair looked like a snowstorm as I soaked one tissue after another after another. The room remained silent as I wept, bent over in deep emotional pain. Thirty-nine years of sorrow and grief and rage and pain and regret all came gushing out like a volcanic eruption.

Finally, *finally*, the volcano flow subsided. I forgave my father, but I didn't know yet that I needed forgiveness *from* my father for the years of hatred I held toward him. Dr. Tan was not finished. He then asked me to keep watching the scene and tell the class what I saw.

The next scene that popped up was my high school graduation, being held in a large gymnasium. As I stood in the front of the line ready to give my valedictory address, I peeked around the large curtain to scan the audience. To my shock, my dad sat in the audience, making a big commotion. He told everyone, "Hey, look! My daughter is first in her class! Look at this (pointing to the printed program). That's my daughter!! I'm so proud of her!"

But, the scene confused me. First, my dad died when I was in seventh grade, so it couldn't have been a real memory. Second, my dad was proud of me? That didn't seem very plausible either. Suddenly the scene changed, and I stood at the end of my graduating class. Instead of having a 4.0 grade point average and graduating first in my class, I was the tail-end of the class. The 17-year-old Beverly I saw in that vision was ashamed and embarrassed. The one thing she was reasonably good at—academics—had suddenly turned into shame and disgrace.

But then Jesus in a flash appeared to me at the tail end of the graduates, took the mortar board off my head, sailed it into the gym rafters, picked me up by the waist, and began twirling me around and around. He kept yelling out at the crowd: "This is my beloved daughter. I am so proud of her."

After He sat me back down on the floor, I began to unravel the meaning of the encounter with Jesus. It didn't matter to Him if I were smart or dull, tall or short, beautiful or plain, talented or ordinary; Jesus loved me no matter what. Unconditional love. I didn't have to perform for Him. I didn't have to be perfect. Or smart. Or athletic. Or musical. Or anything at all! He loved me simply because I was His kid. Period.

"And he that sat upon the throne said, Behold, I make all things new."

Later that night in my retreat bedroom, I made peace with my dad. I forgave him of his misdeeds and omitted deeds. I told him I had missed him growing up, and I wished he could have been part of my adult life. I told him I loved him and that I grieved over his early death. But then, the real transformative work began: *I asked him to forgive my long-held anger and hatred over these 37 years since his death.* I had done as much damage to myself as my dad had done. Through the light of God's unconditional love, I could finally look at the blackness within – a hardened heart imprisoned by my own resentment. But, I couldn't see it until I was in that deep pit of despair over my own guilt.

In all my efforts to forgive my dad over the years, it was like I was trying to save myself from drowning. I was flailing and kicking and screaming – blaming all my problems on my dad. But in so doing, I was preventing God from saving me from drowning. I had to let go of my will; I had to realize I couldn't do it by myself. God had to let me sink to the deepest level of despair – to a place where I had no power to fix myself. In essence, I had to let go and allow God to take me to shore.

In that moment, I saw my own weaknesses, and that allowed me to understand the weaknesses of my dad.

In that session with Dr. Tan, I gave up the struggle to save myself from drowning; I allowed God to save me. When I asked my dad to forgive me, and I felt that he had, I began to laugh. And laugh. And laugh. I heard my own laughter as coming from a little girl enjoying being held in her daddy's arms. We had forgiven each other and tender love was restored between us. I danced in the desert and no one was there except me and my Soul Companion. We danced for hours until I finally fell asleep. And I slept like a baby, cradled in my Father's strong arms.

The next morning at our last teaching session, one of the other participants wanted to share an experience from the night before. He said he had been estranged from his daughter for many years, mainly because of his own obstinate behaviors. But, when he went to his room, he heard a child laughing in the room next-door. He suddenly remembered how he used to play with his daughter; the laughter he heard was hers as they played together. With tears trickling down his cheeks, he told us he was going to make amends with his daughter because he wanted to be a part of her life. He would do whatever it took, for as long as it took, to mend the relationship.

Sandra Wilson, one of the participating psychologists, included my story in her book, *Into Abba's Arms, Finding the Acceptance You've Always Wanted* (Tyndale House, 1998). The leader of the Clinical Institute program, Dr. Gary Moon, later asked me to take part in making a video of my testimony for a Curt Cloninger film series on

"God Views.[5]" That video has been used by many pastors for several years. Countless women have told me that my story helped them to forgive their fathers and move on with their lives. Yes, He continues to make all things new.

DD Day

I started the PhD program in the fall of 1997 and completed it in May 2000. Waves of panic rose up and then fell in my chest and throat as I drove down to Georgia State for the last time. That was the day, the "make it or break it" day. My three years of work—and money—would either hit the jackpot or sink into a black hole. I was about to storm the beach. It was my D Day, well, my DD Day, Dissertation Defense Day – May 1, 2000.

As I drove down I-85 toward Atlanta, my mind went back to the big arguments I had with God about "why should I do this stupid degree, anyway? I don't need it for my social status. I'm 52 years old, so what good is this degree at this point in life?" God had been silent during my profound speeches and rhetorical questions. But I also saw that God wasn't forcing me to do anything. He never does. Instead, He was giving me an opportunity if I wanted it. He did not coerce; He invited me to dance in the desert, and I had merely accepted His invitation.

My one and only thought about a PhD at my age was that God was preparing me to teach at Emmanuel College after I retired from the school system. But, really, I didn't need that degree to do adjunct teaching, which I had already been doing for 10 years.

Still, I couldn't shake the thought that God might have something more for me to do. I had no idea what that might be. Maybe

5 http://lifespringsresources.com/media/wysiwyg/God_Views_Resource_Guide.pdf LifeSprings Resources, God Views Resource Guide

something new. My mind went back to Ken Medema's song, "Dancing in the Desert."

I began chuckling as I drove downtown. I had entered the PhD program merely for the credential of the degree so I could teach. I did not know for a full year into my doctoral studies that I could become licensed as a psychologist with a PhD in psychology. Never crossed my mind. My colleagues in the program were incredulous! "What? You didn't know that? That's the only reason we are in this degree program."

So, now, three years later, a lot more was riding on my dissertation defense than just the degree. Without the degree, I would never become a licensed psychologist.

"Lord, help," I prayed as my car sped down the far left lane toward downtown. "Help me not have a wreck on this last leg of my trip. Help me with the projector for my PowerPoint. Lord, You know technology and I are mortal enemies. Help my mind to be calm and collected as I present my dissertation defense. Help me to not babble like an idiot when my committee members ask tough questions. Help me answer questions about the multivariate analysis of the academic and behavioral correlates of Attention-Deficit/ Hyperactivity Disorder Subtypes and the effect size in my data. Help me not freeze up when Dr. Evans asks me a question I cannot answer. Just help me make up something brilliant."

My dissertation defense was open for anyone to attend. Four or five colleagues came along. I saw a couple of my previous students who were doing degrees at Georgia State. Just what I wanted—friends to watch my demise. My dear Paul had also come for moral support, but he holed up in a room down the hall at my request. No need to add more pressure to my already frazzled nerves.

I did not freeze or flee or laugh uncontrollably as I did in my sixth grade oral speech disaster. As my Soul Companion stood with me, His peace became mine. My confidence and deportment came from Him. I must have answered all questions; I must have looked and sounded PhD-worthy. I did not expect applause at the end, but I got it. I think they applauded because the oldest student in the department actually finished – and finished quicker than anyone else. I explained, "At my age, I have to hurry and pay off my school loans before I kick the bucket and my kids will have to use their inheritance to pay them off. That will give them even more reason to say, 'See, Mom, we told you so… you're too old to go back to school.'" That's not true! Paul and our kids had been very supportive of my crazy midlife adventure. They had taken care of meal times and house cleaning and been without me at recreational times. But, now I could pick up all those chores and none of them would complain.

After the applause, Dr. Evans dismissed me from the room. A few minutes later, he invited me back into the room, shook my hand, and announced, "Congratulations, Dr. Oxley. You did it."

Paul and I celebrated the day by going to Sam's Club for cleaning supplies. But he also bought me a chili dog and frosted orange drink at the Varsity. The celebration dinner would come later that summer. But, I just wanted time to breathe again. I also wanted to clean my house. I hadn't done a good job of that for almost three years. We bought a lot of cleaning supplies that day.

With PhD in hand, Emmanuel College asked me to teach full-time that fall. I explained that I needed to finish three more years in the public schools so I could retire with full benefits. Not sure how it all happened, but both the college and the school system hired me for three-quarters time in each position. I knew I could handle that easily since I was no longer driving to Atlanta twice a week. No more stat courses. No more term papers. No more articles to write for publication. FREEDOM! Sweet freedom. I could dance freely without too many responsibilities to tie me down.

The next three years passed quickly. I retired from public schools in May 2003, after 32 years of service. Now, my life of ease could begin. Only one job to do. A woman of pure leisure. I felt downright lazy. But my life was about to turn deeper into the desert. I didn't know what was coming, but my Soul Companion did. He had planned it all while I was still in my mother's womb.

Beverly, Julinna and Andeena (daughters) at PhD hooding

Chapter 9

Meeting God in Gatlinburg

Those who have lived a few decades know storm damage can be horrific, even deadly. To survive, we have to find protection. But, storms also bring great benefits. For example, storms function like a transport truck, hauling water and lower temperatures to places in desperate need. They cleanse the atmosphere and even unlock buried seed that can change the direction of lives, regions, or nations.

Seeds represent one of God's most mysterious creations. They can remain dry and "dead" for centuries until the right combination of soil and water releases life. Then a green shoot will break through the dirt, reaching for the sun. Another mysterious feature is that seeds never resemble the plant that grows from them. As Paul told the Corinthians, "...what you put in the ground is not the plant that will grow, but only a bare seed of wheat or whatever you are planting."[6]

6 1 Corinthians 15:37 taken from the HOLY BIBLE, NEW LIVING TRANSLATION (NLT): Scriptures taken from the HOLY BIBLE, NEW LIVING TRANSLATION, Copyright© 1996, 2004, 2007 by Tyndale House Foundation. Used by permission of Tyndale House Publishers, Inc., Carol Stream, Illinois 60188. All rights reserved. Used by permission.

In 1984 I realized that God had dropped *something* in my heart through the musical prophecy of Ken Medema. I was clueless about what it meant and, to be honest, after years of seeing no signs of a sprout or anything breaking through the soil, I let the idea of service to my Franklin Springs community slip out of my mind. I forgot about that prophecy. In 2007, another seed planted by Lee Grady foretold that Paul and I would be involved in something brand-new, something that would be resisted, but we would be thrust into it whether we wanted it or not. More on that later.

Both of these withered and dead kernels poked up through the dirt in 2009. But I didn't recognize them until well after they had produced a splendid plant that has continued to beautify the Franklin Springs landscape.

License to Practice

I studied for the licensure exam until my brain waves were smoking, paid good money to take the exam, and then paid the licensure fee—an amount that would purchase a reliable used car. In purely objective terms, all that money and time only produced two pieces of paper to hang on the wall—the 18 X 20 "sheepskin" proclaiming DOCTORATE OF PHILOSOPHY DEGREE from GEORGIA STATE UNIVERSITY and a 3 X 5 plain piece of paper announcing GEORGIA LICENSED PSYCHOLOGIST #002528.

Both pieces of paper tell the public I am qualified to practice on them. Practice? Yes. Those of us in the field of mental (or physical) health *practice* on people every day, hoping something we do is helpful. If it helps, we get to practice on more people. And they may tell others how we helped them. Word of mouth: that's part of building a business around healthcare. If what we practice does not help, we spent a lot of money for nothing because we will soon be out of business.

I had earned another piece of paper, now suitably framed: "Registered Play Therapist." That means I get to play with children and get paid for it. Not a bad deal. OK, not exactly, I don't "play with children." Rather, through the process of play (children's natural language), therapists help children learn to communicate with others, express feelings, develop problem-solving skills, and learn healthy ways of coping and relating to others. In that therapeutic process, play brings healing to emotionally damaged, traumatized, or despondent children. I love it because God has gifted me with a natural way with children. I love them and they (somehow) know it.

One day I realized that although I had impressive looking credentials to hang on the wall, I had no wall. No chair and no office. So, at her invitation, I joined Patty Adkins in her private practice. I hoped I wouldn't harm too many people, especially kids, before I figured out what I was doing. I hoped to see eight to 10 clients per week, teach in the Psychology Department at Emmanuel College, retire again at 65, draw my Social Security, become a grandmother, take cruises to exotic places, and eat bonbons by the pool. My life would be set. I would live happily ever after.

Running into God in Gatlinburg

In 2007, Bane and Barbara James invited Paul and me to one of their Joysprings retreats in Gatlinburg, TN. Author and *Charisma* editor Lee Grady would be teaching with Bane and Barbara. Sure, that sounds fun. We'll slip up into the Smokies, buy some crafts, drive mountain roads, and perhaps meet some nice folks. The whole experience would fit our comfort zones quite nicely.

After a brief session of teaching and fellowship, Grady called Paul and me to the front of the room. Besides being a gifted speaker, writer, and editor, Lee flows in the gift of prophecy. My skepticism kicked in and my comfort zone alarm started wailing.

But it was too late. Lee began to speak to us:

Although his prophecy to us was quite long, the real seed planted that day came in these words: "*They are stepping into the threshold of a bright new day and I am giving them a new assignment and a new anointing; it's a new day. The Lord says you are thermostats... I hear Him say... The temperature is going way up. I've placed you where I've placed you. I will turn up the heat in the whole environment. There will be resistance to what you are doing… they will resist with words, cold shoulders, snubbing, sometimes painful resistance.*

... You will go against tradition and the way it's been for a while.

If you go upstream and against the flow, I'll send reinforcements. Others will join you, and the current is going to change.

I am thrusting you into the midst of this whether you like it or not."

When the retreat concluded two days later, Paul and I drove for miles back home in silence. Finally, I spoke. "Who wants to hear a prophecy like that? God is going to mess up our lives, we'll have lots of opposition, and it will be hard. What's more, we don't have any choice in it—He will throw us into deep water whether we like it or not. AND, it's going to happen quickly… very soon!"

As we talked, we couldn't imagine even one scenario which would fulfill that kind of prophecy. We quietly tucked it away and put it to bed, hopefully never to remember it again. Back in our routine, we picked up our responsibilities and carried on life as usual. But a seed doesn't care if you forget about it. Once it falls into the dirt, it takes on a life of its own. As the Bible says in Mark 4:26-28, "A man scatters seed on the ground. Night and day, whether he sleeps or gets up, *the seed sprouts and grows, though he does not know how. All by itself the soil produces grain*—first the stalk, then the head, then the full kernel in the head." (italics mine) A storm was rolling in, but we didn't see it. Looking back, it was a good thing we didn't know about it or we might have tried to avert it.

Paul and I continued with our lives. But, as we slept, taught, counseled, led mission trips, and spent time with friends and family, somewhere out in the field, a seed cracked open, and a new sprig of life pushed toward the surface. We didn't see it or even think about it. God didn't care. He knew that when the stalk, the head, and then the full kernel appeared, we could not ignore it any longer.

Meanwhile, my eight to 10 client load per week grew to 25 a week. That is considered full-time work in private practice. Then I started seeing 30 and more clients a week, teaching at Emmanuel in the mornings and doing therapy from 1 p.m. to 9 p.m. Once again, I had two full-time jobs. How did that happen? I simply could not turn away children whose lives had been ravished by environmental and human forces. I had to help them if I could.

"You need some help!"

By that time, I served as Emmanuel College's Psychology Department Chair, which meant I could somewhat arrange my teaching schedule to accommodate my private practice. Teaching morning classes and seeing children and families in the afternoon and evening seemed to be a perfect arrangement for everyone. I could use my teaching theory in my practice and use illustrations from my practice in my classes. Hand in glove. Perfect fit.

Predictably, I burned out. I had been serving many children in foster care because other mental health professionals were not qualified or did not want to be burdened with them. I really couldn't blame them. Foster care is complex—therapists work with the foster parents, biological parents, caseworkers, attorneys, guardians-ad-litem (court-appointed guardians), CASA (court-appointed special advocates), and others in the court system. I was continually subpoenaed to court for judges to hear my recommendations for children. The judges almost always heeded my recommendations, so I knew God had given me favor.

One ordinary day, I sat at a child's round red table in my small rented counseling office with a 5-year-old girl in foster care. We were using play dough. "Carla" (not her real name) suddenly looked up at me and asked, "Do you work here all by yourself?"

I had never been asked that question by anyone, let alone a child.

"Yes, I work here by myself."

"I mean, *all* by yourself?"

"Yes, I do."

She said it again, "ALL by yourself?"

My voice raised: "Yes, I DO! I work here ALL BY MYSELF!" She looked intently at me and said, "Well, you need some help!"

I laughed out loud. I don't know what that little girl saw that made her think I needed help, but she was right; I desperately needed help. I took Carla as a messenger from God. I needed to expand my practice. I could not continue the pace I had kept the past few years. But, how?

When two friends in the field said they would join me if I could find space to rent, I immediately started looking for office space. But, after scouring Franklin Springs and Royston, I knew nothing existed that was suitable for three or four practitioners.

Then someone suggested, "Why don't you just build a counseling center?" That question came out as casually as, "Why don't you just serve ice cream for dessert?"

Build a counseling center? Paul and I had refurbished every house we ever lived in. But we had never even built a birdhouse, much less a counseling and office complex. After a few more months rolled on, we consulted with our friend Brian James, Director of Development at Emmanuel College and the mayor of Franklin Springs, about needing office space. He suggested we consider buying property in Franklin Springs and constructing a facility to meet our needs. He assured us there would be professionals to help us build it.

At the suggestion of building within the city limits of Franklin Springs, I remembered a second prophetic song that Ken Medema composed on that weekend in 1984, one that planted new seeds of destiny in my heart. Although I had forgotten them, those seeds fell into the soil and slept until they were ready to sprout. Twenty-three years later, they opened into my life's calling to bring healing to abused and discouraged children as a child psychologist. It was a vision of what the Franklin Springs community was designed to be:

I have this vision … here's what I see. I see a town, and all around the town,
I see fountains, beautiful fountains.
I see fountains rising up into the air. And the spray from the fountains makes everything bright.
I see ***wells*** *bubbling up from the ground,* ***springs of water*** *shooting high into the sky. Everyone who is thirsty, come to the springs without money, without pride.*
The people there are the gentlest folk you know, loving folks; they will take you in and love you deep. …

They are learning how to live and learning how to love.
I see people coming from Atlanta, Savannah, Florida, Chicago, and New York.
To see the miracle of Franklin Springs. …
This is my vision; this is my dream.

And so, I'll make a pilgrimage to a place I've never been.
I'll go looking for the water.
I'll go looking for small things.
I'll go looking for my healing.
In the springs of Franklin Springs . . .

The Springs cannot be contained; they are bursting from the ground.
Come down, Jesus, like a summer rain; dry deserts we are.
Make the fountains flow again.
Come down, Jesus; like waters of a spring.
Make the fountains flow again and teach us how to sing.
Come down, Jesus. Cause we've been waiting a long, long time.[7]

In 1984 God moved my heart beyond anything I had felt in a very long time. And I knew that, one day, I would be part of the healing waters which pilgrims would come searching for in Franklin Springs. That day had come – 23 years later!

Through major and minor miracles, we built the counseling center in five months. Paul served as the General Contractor; I was his General Flunky. And we both continued teaching full time at Emmanuel, plus my full client load. We opened Wellsprings Psychological Resources on November 15, 2009. My office staff consisted of two persons, Heather Scranton and Judy Henzel. Heather ran the entire office. Judy did the billing. But, I was still the only therapist in that 4,000-square-foot building with nine counseling rooms. For various reasons those associates who wanted to join me could not do so for a while. I worked by myself for nine months.

7 Used by permission, Ken Medema Music, www.kenmedema.com.

Wellsprings Psychological Resources

In retrospect, I see it was best that I had no one else working with me. I had to learn to be a business owner. Up to that point in my life, I had been a special education teacher, school psychologist, college teacher, and a licensed psychologist. But, in November 2009, I became a CEO of a business. And I had no clue what that meant.

That's when God sent Wendy Vinson to me. She had worked in the Christian nonprofit world for several years and knew the ropes of business. When she asked me about a business plan, logo, mission statement, policy and procedure manual, and many other questions, I just looked at her with blank stares. I'm sure she thought, "Wow; this is gonna be a long boat ride."

But Wendy was patient. Soon, I had a logo, stationery, a mission statement, business cards, and I had figured out how to write a policy and procedure manual. Wendy even helped me with employee contracts that would keep me out of trouble. I found (and still hold) deep admiration for that woman.

A few months later, my first post-doc intern came to work. Two months later, a psychologist friend came. Two months later, another friend. Wellsprings Psychological Resources hit the map in our corner of Georgia. Referrals poured in. Wellsprings was earning a good reputation and a wide one. People drove up to 30 - 45 minutes to see us. A few clients came from Atlanta. Over the next few years, we had more therapists than offices. "Carla's" message to me — "You need some help!"— produced a team. And we also had more referrals than our therapists could handle. We were averaging 100 – 125 *new* referrals a month, with our full-time and part-time therapists operating at capacity most of the time. We rented space across the parking lot, which provided two more offices and two more playrooms. I saw healing waters flow to that area again.

Storm Front

Paul and I (and my whole staff) knew we had found favor with the community, but we also encountered opposition, just as Lee Grady had prophesied. When an insurance audit hit Wellsprings, it turned into a five-month ordeal. I later learned they targeted us because of our high volume of work with low-income clients. Of course, we did. We were one of the few providers in northeast Georgia who took those clients. We serve an impoverished region of the state.

During those five months of audit, I spent every weekend at the practice getting all the paperwork together for every claim submitted. I felt like quitting. When it was all over, we had lost over $15,000. I had to dip into personal savings to make payroll and took no (or reduced) salary for several months.

But God kept Wellsprings afloat, and we kept our heads and didn't throw in the towel. I knew Wellsprings was doing wonderful work with children and families. And we followed the rules and guidelines to the best of our knowledge. We made some errors, yes, but relatively few and relatively minor. It didn't matter to the insurer. I sometimes wondered if the insurance companies looked for ways to avoid paying us or to take back money they had already paid. My focus has always been on doing what was right in the eyes of God. He was the One I cared about pleasing. My mantra was to run the practice "above reproach." When we finished the audit, we celebrated by giving gratitude to God for helping us get through the ordeal and to become even better therapists and more meticulous record-keepers.

So, to recap, two years before Wellsprings was built, through Lee Grady's spoken word, a seed fell into the ground of our hearts in Gatlinburg. Then we forgot about it. That didn't matter; the seed grew "all by itself." It was indeed "a new assignment from God" and undeniably "we had to go against tradition and against the flow." But others had joined us in our fervent effort to reverse the downward spiral of America's depravity. And, yes, "we were thrust into it whether we liked it or not." Then, when there was no available office space, we had no choice but to build a counseling center. But, look what that seed had been producing, a flourishing place of our Father's magnificent care. He has been faithful. I often wonder what He has planned for the future of His cherished children? In 2013, He gave me a glimpse of that future. And it scared me half to death!

Of course, other storms came along, some so personal and painful that they cannot be told. However, the ropes that tied me to the mast held me and our staff and clients securely through every storm. Furthermore, every one of the storms served as a healing agent in the lives of my clients. They all somehow knew I understood their plight because I have also been through pain and suffering. Maybe not the same kind they faced, but those who have endured adversity can always spot it in others.

Perhaps even more so, when our clients sense they have a therapist who has been to dreadful places before them, they grant me and other therapists the holy space in our relationship that permits us to speak words of life and hope into their heart. Although they may not understand the source, they hear and receive the same sacred Voice that speaks "peace, be still" to nature and to people.

Chapter 10

Build an Ark!

As a child psychologist, I see clearly how disorders, diseases, and maladaptive behaviors are passed down to the next generation. Some are genetic. For example, according to the Addiction Center, "Research shows that genes are responsible for about half of the risk for AUD [alcohol use disorder]. Therefore, genes alone do not determine whether someone will develop AUD. Environmental factors, as well as gene and environment interactions account for the remainder of the risk."[8]

In short, genetic science clearly shows that alcoholics can pass a *predisposition* toward alcohol abuse to their children. Drug addicts can pass a *predisposition* of addiction on to their offspring. And then there are the behaviors that are environmentally transmitted through modeling: Violence often begets violence. The abused may become abusers. Dysfunctional parents can produce dysfunctional children. Suicidal parents may have suicidal children.

But, psychologists have learned through genetic science that, although a genetic predisposition may be passed down to offspring, children do not become alcoholics if they drink responsibly or choose

8 "Alcohol Addiction and Genetics." Addiction Center Genetics of Alcoholism, December 5, 2019. https://www.addictioncenter.com/alcohol/genetics-of-alcoholism/

not to drink at all. The same is true for many other genetic predispositions. Perhaps the "sins of the fathers being punished to the third and fourth generations" (Numbers 14:17-18) refers to these genetic predispositions.

From my practice, I have a front row seat at the heartbreaking drama of generational curses. Naturally, I feel compelled to do what I can to break the curses, change negative behaviors, bring healing, and help rescue and restore children and parents. Just as God called Noah to build an ark to save people in his day, in 2013 God called me to establish a nonprofit ministry, *The Ark Family Preservation Center*, to save lives through the coming flood.

A Tsunami of Historic Dimensions

Since 1970 I have come to know something profoundly disturbing in my work with children and families - first as a special education teacher in public schools, then as a school psychologist, later as a college professor, and now a licensed psychologist: I see a massive tsunami racing toward our shores.

I am not alone in seeing this fast-approaching deadly storm. The consequences of the current pandemic of the coronavirus (COVID-19) upon the mental health in America is alarming. In a recent PBS News interview, Congressman Patrick Kennedy from Rhode Island used the term "tsunami" to describe the coming mental health crisis. He urged us to be prepared for the surge in depression, addictions and suicides. I see the same storm, but I probably see it more as a consequence of the collapse of moral standards and civility in people.

Almost 30 years ago, a novel told us, "Damaged people are dangerous. They know they can survive."[9] In other words, damaged

9 Josephine Hart, *Damage* (Alfred A. Knoph, New York, 1991)

people damage others. They pass on the pain they absorbed. Yes, I know incest, rape, and murder of children have always afflicted society. But today's scourge of drugs—methamphetamines, opioids, and other substances—has brought mountainous enabling of truly horrid behavior, thereby metastasizing its evil. As I have seen, that evil seeps down through generations; the children of addicts become addicts, school dropouts begat dropouts, the abused become abusers, on and on, generation after generation.

Wendell Berry sees the same condition, but describes it differently. He writes, "The modern urban-industrial society is based on a series of radical disconnections between body and soul, husband and wife, marriage and community, community and the earth . . . Together, these disconnections add up to a condition of critical ill health which we suffer in common."[10] Social scientists and other professionals sometimes refer to the disconnections as alienation, overwhelming loneliness, even weariness of life. But those academic words camouflage the demonic, putrid, and heartbreaking details of sexual abuse, domestic violence, and addictions. That storm has already started rearranging the coastlines of our society.

These raging storms have been tearing families apart for a long time, and the destruction is now increasing. As I have worked with clients over the years, I have noticed changing trends in our rural society that are prevalent across the United States.

In my practice where we serve an out-patient clinical population, I have *rarely* seen a nuclear, intact family—a biological mother and father and their children. Perhaps one family in 20 that presents for therapy is not divorced or blended or has a single parent. Thus, in this rural

10 Wendell Berry, *The Art of the Commonplace* (Washington, DC, Shoemaker & Hoard, 2002)

clinical population, a large majority of children are now living in single-parent homes or with step-parents, live-in partners, or grandparents.

Nationwide, over 10% of American children live with their grandparents, but in my practice, about half of the children coming to us live with their grandparents, other relatives, or are in foster care. The number one reason for these children not living with their parents is drug and alcohol abuse, including the pandemic of opioid abuse.

According to the Centers for Disease Control and Prevention (CDC), "In 2017, more than 70,000 people died from drug overdoses (almost 50,000 of those from opiate overdoses), making it a leading cause of injury-related death in the United States."[11]

The destructive addictions, especially recreational drugs, are intensifying dramatically. While drug usage seemed to level off in the 1990s, it has again spun out of control with the latest epidemic of poly-drug abuse, especially among teenagers. The most common drugs being used together are cocaine, heroin, prescription stimulants, benzodiazepines, and opioids. Effects of poly-drug abuse? Brain damage, coma, seizures, stroke, and respiratory failure, all of which can result in death.

These tempests have also been escalating hideous sexual abuse. Perhaps the most common reason children are brought into foster care is for sexual abuse. Children who have been raped by a father figure or a mother figure will require months or even years of therapy to work through their trauma. My role as a psychologist requires me to notify Georgia's Division of Family and Children Services (DFCS) to report such cases. The atrocities reach such magnitude that they're too staggering to *know*, let alone communicate to others.

11 "America's Drug Overdose Epidemic: Data to Action (Centers for Disease Control and Prevention)," America's Drug Overdose Epidemic: Data to Action. https://www.cdc.gov/injury/features/prescription-drug-overdose/index.html

Sadly, the foster care system is escalating with so many referrals that they can only respond to the most horrific cases—those children who are so badly sexually abused or chronically neglected that their lives are in danger. An average of four children a day die in America from abuse and neglect.

In the Trenches

In order for you, the reader, to understand the damage projected from the coming tsunami, come down into the trenches with me. In my public-school experience, I worked primarily with children and only occasionally with their parents. When I opened a private practice, I began working with the entire family system. And I had to descend into their world in order to show them a way up to healing. The depth of depravity shocked me to my core. I felt like Chief Brody (Roy Scheider) in *Jaws* when his face-to-face encounter with the shark blew him back from the edge of the boat in stark terror. I also identify with his line, "You're gonna need a bigger boat." America needs a fleet of bigger boats to deal with what's coming.

Consider a mother pleading for help to get over the pain of losing her daughter in a head-on collision caused by another driver checking her cell-phone. I couldn't stand at the top of the ridge and yell instructions to her on how to grieve and "just get over it." I had to go down where she had sunk. I had to weep with her and pray with her. She had no faith for her future. But, months later, with God's help, she was able to climb high enough out of that hole to resume her life with her husband and other children. Her grief will go on, but she can now get out of bed in the morning.

When parents came to me in deep agony over the death of their drug-addicted son, I could not remain detached; I had to sit in the ashes with them.

When a preteen was raped by her mother's boyfriend and became mute out of sheer terror, I entered her world of dark silence. And I stayed until she trusted me to walk with her into the light. When she did, her voice returned and her spirit was healed.

When a family presented for therapy after the suicide of their father, I had to go down into their emotional pit to carry Jesus' words of life and hope. It was vitally important to me to try to prevent the actions of the father from being passed down to his children. Healing those wounds was critical to stopping the vicious cycle of self-destruction.

I know too well what can happen at night in homes that should be safe havens for children. The dark of night covers so much sexual violation. That's the prime time for such tragic behavior. And alcohol and drugs come into the scene to make vile behavior appear "acceptable." I recently worked with children whose father shot and killed their mother and then himself. They suffered unbelievable heartaches as they adjusted to life as orphans. Someone had to get down into the trenches with those little ones to help them understand what had happened to their parents. And I prayed for God to heal their shattered lives and scarred hearts.

I have only shared a glimpse of the horrors so you can understand the stakes for America and her children and parents. Of course, I have protected the confidentiality and privacy of the clients involved. But, it's critically important that we as a society begin to understand more fully the degenerate and hellish depths of danger to children. And that reveals the vital need for good mental health care.

Feed my Sheep

When I entered private practice in 2003, I had 33 years' experience in public school education. I thought I had a good foundation to build upon as I entered a new phase of service to God and His little ones. But, I had no idea. I felt like someone who had been taking my ship on harbor tours for 33 years. Then, I was jerked onto a small and damaged warship in a desperate fight against great and savage odds. Had I known where my professional voyage would take me I may have jumped ship early on.

In 2013 I responded to the Spirit's voice to "feed my sheep." I knew He was directing me to launch a nonprofit ministry for the foster care population and other families in crisis, even those without means to pay. I saw that the plethora of needs in my niche in northeast Georgia surpassed the scope and capacities of what Wellsprings Psychological Resources could handle. Wellsprings is a "for-profit" (a legal IRS category) counseling center, meaning that we serve clients with insurance or can self-pay, even on a sliding fee scale. But, what about those who can't pay? Those who have no resources to get critical care? Those who don't qualify for mental health care?

And what about those who need services beyond insurance coverage? For example, insurance doesn't cover supervised visitation. Or anger management classes. Or parenting classes. Or grief support. All of those programs have proven effective when executed by qualified professionals. But, if people cannot pay for those services, what good are they? That leaves those in desperate need as "sheep without a shepherd." They have no one to feed or care for them.

In April, 2013, I took my first step in responding to the tsunami. I invited a wide range of professionals to a forum hosted at Wellsprings. The participants represented centers of child abuse, domestic violence, CASA (court-appointed special advocates), drug rehabilitation, and foster care. The group also included attorneys working with the foster care system and adoption agencies, educators in public and private schools, pastors of local churches, and foster parents. Virtually all 20+ attendees that day saw the same glaring deficiencies in services in northeast Georgia. The cry that rose up out of that forum reverberated in my ears long after the meeting was over: *Our society faces historic waves of destruction.* I knew God wanted me to do something about it. At least, I had to try!

The professionals gathered that day commended the work of Wellsprings. But, they also recognized that something more was needed. One of the most urgent needs expressed that day was for a visitation center where a child, say, in foster care could see his or her biological parents in a safe place. Such visitations can be very valuable. *And volatile.* So courts get involved with the visits. For example, sometimes when a parent gets released from prison or successfully completes a drug rehabilitation program, a judge will issue a court order granting their request for visitation with their child. But where and how could such a visitation take place, a place that assures safety, order, cleanliness, and peace?

In our rural area, some of those "supervised visits" have taken place in fast food restaurants. But without money to buy food, the family is often asked to leave the premises. So they end up in the parking lot. Or they may go to a public park or a library. If the visits take place at the DFCS office, the caseworkers have neither the time nor expertise to provide the coaching needed to teach parenting skills.

In that 2013 forum of Franklin County professionals, we heard widespread agreement that a visitation center was needed that included coaching for the parents. In this model, parents could observe "best practices" for good parenting skills. Helping these clients with mental health issues would require The Ark to also provide anger management classes, support groups for grief and suicide, support groups for grandparents raising grandchildren, and on and on. So many needs, so few resources.

I believed we could provide an effective, clean, and safe visitation center if we could find the resources to build and maintain it. Working together with other agencies, we could *start* to repair the disconnected relationships, break generational curses of addiction, alcoholism, abuse, homelessness, and unemployment. We could help slow (perhaps even reverse) the family breakdowns in our community. I could not allow these people to keep falling through societal cracks without at least trying to help them escape their desperate conditions! I wanted to help give access to a better life for their children.

Time for Action

It seemed like God was saying to me, "Are you just going to keep talking about it or will you actually *do* something and reach out your hand to my suffering children? It's time to act! Get up and do something about these atrocities all around you. If you love Me, feed my sheep." I was reminded of Edmund Burke's quote (although it was directed toward the American government in 1770, it pertains to us today): "*The only thing necessary for the triumph of evil is for good men to do nothing.*"

A fire began to burn within me. I invited two of my close friends, Paula Dixon and Wendy Vinson, to pray with me; I had to discern God's plan for how to help this underserved population. They have acted as my "Aaron and Hur" for more than seven years, as of this writing, faithfully upholding my arms in prayer when I have been beleaguered or discouraged. (Ex. 17:12 tells how Aaron and Hur held up Moses' hands when they grew tired, one on one side and one on the other, so that his hands remained steady until sunset so that Joshua could defeat the Amalekites with his sword.)

In the summer of 2013 Paul and I took the first step and bought land next to Wellsprings for the development of The Ark Family Preservation Center. I wrote the application for nonprofit status in September 2013 and received an approval letter on January 8, 2014 (a process that normally takes a year).

A Board of Directors for The Ark was formed and got to work. We offered anger management and parenting classes. Within a few months, we rented a place across the street from Wellsprings for supervised visits to noncustodial parents; trained coaches were present at all times. Judges began making court-ordered referrals to us. The Ark was able to provide for all these services with private party donations.

Grandma Clinkenbeard

The response quickly surpassed our available space. So, in the fall of 2014, The Ark board launched a capital campaign to raise money for a building on the land we donated to the nonprofit. When one of the board members suggested I lead the campaign, I remembered my dislike for public speaking – in my sixth grade class, in graduate school, and even now. But, my Soul Companion reminded me that all I needed to do was to share His vision of The Ark and He would do the rest. Paul and I are convinced that God called The Ark into existence.

My first appeal was to my cousins to support the development of a centerpiece garden in honor of our Grandmother Clinkenbeard who loved to give away her flowers and vegetables as much as she enjoyed growing them. To date, my cousins along with a few other donors have given almost $20,000 to create walking paths with raised flower beds, benches, statuary, a birdbath, and other items to enhance the therapeutic value of God's natural landscapes.

Members of Paul's family, my family, and some wonderful donors in the community have joined in the vision to see a building constructed. We don't have enough money to build a facility yet, so we wait. We wait for God to show us where to go from here.

Teachers in our local school system understand the stakes. They stand on the front lines of that war. That's why they have chosen to make monthly donations through payroll deductions. In fact, at the time of this writing, the teachers' financial support provides about 33% of the income for the services provided by The Ark.

Writing grants is another stream of support for us. With the help of Liz Gilchrest, one of my capable Wellsprings therapists, we have received grants for scholarships supporting the supervised visits, a basketball court, and wrought-iron fencing to surround it. We've also built a therapeutic playground with a Noah's Ark play set centerpiece. The place now features curved sidewalks, rock retaining walls, swing sets, picnic table, benches, and a lovely lawn of Zoysia grass, manicured by professional landscapers.

Functioning as the director and heading the campaign to raise money for The Ark presents the greatest professional challenge I've yet faced. Every payroll stretches my faith. But I know when we navigate according to God's leading, He will show us the next thing to do. And the next. I can't look too far ahead. He doesn't guide me that way. But I can trust Him to lead. One step at a time. Noah took decades to build The Ark. I bet he got discouraged at times, but he kept on building. He knew a flood was on its way. He did his best to warn his friends and family about it and to build a means of survival.

I'm trying to do the same thing.

Noah's Ark and The Ark Park

Chapter 11

Passing the Torch

These days I often feel like a pioneer, standing on a ridge, gazing back at the crooked trail that brought me to this "scenic overlook" of my life. Standing at such a high place helps us see the larger view of what God really did in that meandering path.

As Moses stood on Mount Nebo at the end of his life, he too looked back and remembered the power, kindness, and faithfulness of His God. From that place, God showed him all the land, sweeping from the Jericho River below his feet, clear to the Mediterranean. In fact, he saw all the land God gave to Abraham and his descendants. Although Moses saw the land, he could not take his people there. So he laid his hands on Joshua, whom he had trained, and commissioned him to lead the Israelites into the Promised Land.

Passing the Torch

Life is often like a relay team; we receive the torch from those preceding us, carry it as well as we can, and then hand it off to the next generation.

Moses mentored Joshua well. As a result, he was well equipped and trained to become Israel's next leader. He became a man of great courage and "was filled with the spirit of wisdom when Moses laid hands on him" (Deut. 34:9). God's word to Joshua is a word to all of us who have received the torch from previous runners: "As I was with Moses, so I will be with you. I will never leave you nor forsake you" (Joshua 1:5).

To the Next Generation of Therapists

As a professional, I have tried to pass the torch to those who would carry it with skill and integrity and run with all their might. Some have dropped it, but more have picked it up and run like the wind. I look for endurance, curiosity, and a desire to learn. I believe allowing newbies to see and join all aspects of the profession—the good, the bad, the ugly—is essential. I've never been afraid to let them see my flaws as well as my strengths. I want them to know and understand the struggle. Leadership requires authenticity and vulnerability. I also believe and practice training, honest assessment, re-training, more honest assessment, all the while building more and more confidence in their decisions and work.

From student teachers to school psychology trainees to interns in private practice, I have had the privilege of coaching five decades of apprentices – more than 50 so far. To date, I have trained 18 interns at Wellsprings and have encouraged my colleagues to train them as well. Investing in the next generation is fulfilling and challenging. More than that, it is essential work.

My professional training has been in client-centered, Adlerian, and experiential play therapy, including sandtray therapy[12] used with

12 Sandtray therapy is an expressive play process which utilizes "images" (miniature toys) in dry or wet sandtrays. The client uses these images to communicate a story or illustrate emotions for the purpose of resolving psychosocial difficulties. It is particularly effective for clients whose trauma has been buried but needs to be brought to consciousness so it can be resolved and the client can live a more productive life. This type therapy bypasses the language center of the left hemisphere of the brain by accessing the right side of the brain where visual-spatial data are stored. Often, during

older children and adults. But, I don't use any one therapy template. There are as many therapeutic approaches as there are clients. Since each client is unique, each requires a unique therapy. That's because psychotherapy is more of an art than a science.

The goal of the therapist is to be fully emotionally present with the client so the client feels understood, respected, cared for. That sacred relationship is where healing takes place. At Wellsprings, we provide the encouragement, training, feedback, freedom, and safe spaces where interns can discover who they are and what kind of therapist God has destined them to become.

At Wellsprings we encourage *all* employees to be authentic, self-disclosing, and kind to themselves and others. We invite everyone to be honest, to disagree, to be free thinking, and to laugh. Good-natured humor carries healing throughout the office environment. We are a family committed to protecting each other's backs. We're a team; when a member needs help, the other team members jump in to serve. We see ourselves as wounded healers—the most effective of therapists.

And, that, boys and girls, is what passing the torch to a new generation of professionals looks like. I didn't read a manual or watch a video series on how to do that, but rather allowed God to breathe life into our relationships.

To the Next Generation of Family

Once I worked through the wounds left over from my childhood and gained a broader perspective of my life, I came to appreciate my family of origin. I am aware that I would not have become who I am today without the seeds planted by my father and mother. And I'm sure I

the "discussion" phase of the sandtray scene, there is an "ah-ha" moment that sheds light on the issue and allows the healing process to begin. I witness miracles of healing almost every time this sacrosanct type of therapy is used.

inherited my father's capacity for dreaming big dreams and generosity and Mom's grit and graciousness.

Despite the pain and turmoil of their own lives, the Harris and Clinkenbeard families were authentic people of fortitude who did the best they could to serve God. As I finally came to accept later in life, Mom's seriousness and Dad's lightheartedness created a good mix for me. That blend helped me to find balance as a wife, mother, grandmother, friend, teacher, and therapist. I benefit from those who have run the race before me.

Naturally, I try to pass the family torch to our two daughters. Julinna, a professor of philosophy at Coastal Carolina University, is a generous, compassionate, honest, conscientious, and achieving woman. Although she and I often take different sides of political issues, we love and respect each other too much to allow different viewpoints to

Julinna, PhD, Professor of Philosophy, Coastal Carolina University

Andeena, MSW, MBA – Director of Financial Services, Wellsprings

separate us. Relationships are more important than opinions. Julinna's influence spreads beyond her students and friends into the community as she organizes worthy causes and supports women and minorities whose rights have been violated. She teaches her two daughters to care about those issues too.

Andeena's passion is primarily for animals and people pushed to the margins of society. Throughout her life, she has cared for the elderly, served the foster care population, and rescued many cats and dogs, which ended up in her parents' care. In so doing she taught Mom and Dad the value of loving and caring for some of man's best friends. And, despite her objection to math in school, she has worked as my billing and financial manager for most of Wellsprings' history. I call her our "ethics taskmaster" because of her stern insistence on ethical and efficient coding and paperwork completion.

Now, I pray that my descendants, especially my two granddaughters Marigny and Parisa, will carry the torch of godly character and devotion, continuing the race in their generation, as they passionately pursue whatever service God calls them to. That will be my greatest reward.

I often think of my Grandma Clinkenbeard on her 90th birthday. As I encouraged her to live to her 100th birthday so she could be our family's first centenarian, she quipped, "Oh, no! I don't want to live to be 100. I want to die while I am still young." What a brilliant view of living young. And she was right. The Bible says "Moses was a hundred and twenty years old when he died, yet his eyes were not weak nor his strength gone."[13] The Message translates the last part of that verse as, "... His eyesight was sharp; he still walked with a spring in his step."[14] We should remain ever young in spirit with a fresh vibrancy as we explore the majestic possibilities of what God wants to do with our lives.

Will and Ariel Durant cast a fine light for our path when they wrote, "Civilization is not inherited; it has to be learned and earned by each generation anew; if the transmission should be interrupted ... civilization would die, and we should be savages again." [15]

The Dominoes

So often life events can be like a long line of standing dominoes. Like dominoes, life events do not exist in isolation, but rather in relationship with other decisions. Often, 1 leads to 2, the second to the third, and so

13 Deuteronomy 34:7

14 THE MESSAGE: THE BIBLE IN CONTEMPORARY ENGLISH (TM): Scripture taken from THE MESSAGE: THE BIBLE IN CONTEMPORARY ENGLISH, copyright©1993, 1994, 1995, 1996, 2000, 2001, 2002. Used by permission of NavPress Publishing Group

15 Will and Ariel Durant, *The Lessons of History* (New York; Simon & Schuster, 1968)

on. At the end of your life, you may be amazed at how God networked events and decisions at critical points in your journey when you were least aware of them. When the first domino falls, it sets off a long chain reaction.

I believe God has overseen every mile and every minute of my life. Even when I overstepped boundaries, He allowed me freedom to fail or transgress. I am not a robot, programmed to do His bidding. I am free to accept or reject Him. I can freely love or hate or be unconcerned. He gives us complete freedom of choice in the matter. But, when we do cooperate with His divine purpose, His plan unfolds in consequential ways before our very eyes. I don't imply that we will always be blessed with wealth or health or fame. Often, those superficial gauges are not blessings at all – they can be traps set by the enemy of our soul. Contrary to much contemporary Christian thought, martyrs who have given their lives for Christ attest to the greatest blessing of all – the sacred gift of sacrificing their lives for His cause.

So, from where I stand now, looking back on the journey of my life, I am astonished to see how God lined up all the dominoes with such great care and design. Sometimes they fell slowly, tottering before falling, and sometimes they bolted toward the finish line.

I learned subtle changes can bring profound results. Because sailing vessels can get swept off course in high winds and waves, they continually course-correct to reach their destination. Sometimes that adjustment may require miniscule change, perhaps only 1 degree or less, in order to sail into the intended harbor. But, without that small modification, the ship may never reach its destination.

Some of these life events fall into the category of personal decisions. But, I also know I have lived my life in the palm of His Hand. So, yes, I believe He influenced these decisions. Although this part will probably speak more to my family than other readers, every life knows its own line of dominoes. So, maybe by reading mine, you will catch some insight into your own. Perhaps I share them as a way of asking you to *pay attention*, be purposeful in your life, and show up ready for your own adventure!

1. Choosing my Captain

   I made my first (and most important) decision at age 9. I tied myself to the mast and asked God to become Captain of my ship. That decision led naturally to other pivotal decisions, commitments that have defined my life. When I was seized by the power of a great affection on that Sunday morning at age 9, I had no idea that it would chart the entire course of my life.

2. Choosing College

   In an era that didn't see as many students go to college, my fifth grade teacher, Mrs. Sauer, planted the idea of a college education in my young brain. And those seeds germinated throughout high school. While most of my friends made wedding plans during their senior year, I made college plans. While they spent money on wedding dresses, I was earning money to pay for the ACT test and application fees for college.

   Mrs. Sauer saw something in me that caused her to speak words of life into my parched spirit. She believed in me and demonstrated it by spending extra time with me, getting to know my past and my fears. When I was a teacher in K-12 schools and in college, I also tried to spend quality time with students, helping them discover their God-given talents, and encouraging them toward a purpose-driven life.

3. Choosing ORU

   Anyone choosing to go to college quickly faces a new question: Where? I wanted excellence in the college, but one anchored in a Christian perspective and culture. I knew Oral Roberts

University had emerged from a vision of greatness. As a result, they attracted many students like me who cared about quality and social environment.

So, the domino of choosing college tumbled right into a Christian education, which tumbled into ORU. And that one led to the next.

4. Choosing Paul

   I knew that Paul was rock solid in his faith in God and in his commitment to me. His faithfulness *to* me and his faith *in* me, transcended all my doubts and anxieties. And our marriage produced two daughters, two granddaughters, and linked a vast web of the Harris, Oxley, and Clinkenbeard families. Just as I supported Paul's career and interest in mission work over the years, he has championed my professional endeavors. I know very few husbands who would give so sacrificially in time and money for their wives' ministries. He's a unique man as all who know him will verify.

5. Choosing the Field of Special Education

   The decision to teach special education placed me in the midst of children who lived on the edges of convention. For reasons of social blindness and bias, children who were "different" faced challenges most of us could not possibly consider. And I've continued to walk further into their world for the 50 years since I taught my first students with special needs. That choice created a thematic continuity with the whole of my life.

6. Moving to Georgia

   Through God's direction, we left family, job, home, friends, church, everything, and moved to Franklin Springs, Georgia. Although that decision (as marital decisions often do) focused more on my spouse (Paul's service as a teacher at Emmanuel

College), it opened the widest doors of opportunity I could ever have imagined. *Because we moved to Georgia,* I found the grace, energy, and anointing to take mission teams to Israel, East Africa, Eastern Europe, Western Europe, and Asia. The falling dominoes picked up speed.

Because of our connections with Emmanuel, Paul and I led premarital classes for engaged couples in our home for several years. I was given leadership positions in our local church and on the general church Board of Publications and the Polity Committee. And, because I was living in a rural area with limited resources, I was given a wide range of disabilities in my teaching assignments in the public schools.

Perhaps one of the greatest blessings of living in Georgia in the Franklin Springs community, I had access to the vast resources of Christian leaders who came to Emmanuel College and the Franklin Springs Church over the years; I was exposed to spiritual formation and the integration of faith and learning. These ideas, novel to me, made me hunger for deeper truths found in both the historical writings of our Christian faith and the fresh new waves of the charismatic movement.

7. Moving to Kenya

   We as a family enjoyed a rare opportunity to live in Kenya for a year. That move allowed me to provide workshops on the effects of trauma on children and other psychological topics in Nairobi, Kenya. I also taught courses at the Eldoret Bible school in Kenya.

8. Taking Special Education to Kenya

   At the request of the Director of an orphanage and private school in Eldoret, Kenya, I established a special education program (that continues). Today, those students lead fruitful lives because they were educated to their potential.

9. Exploring Other Oases of Spiritual Formation
   Enrolling in Gary Moon's Institute of Clinical Theology became a new portal of life for me. For example, I began going to the monastery once or twice a year for weekend spiritual retreats. I have continued that practice for 23 years. My spiritual walk deepened just by living in the presence of Cistercian monks and participating in their "liturgy of the hours" five times a day. We practiced total silence except during the liturgies and the mass. I heard God speak more clearly in my silent time there than perhaps any other place. I have maintained my membership in the denomination of my birth, while benefiting immensely from the ecumenical church.
10. Forgiving My Father and My Father Forgiving Me
    Forgiving my father, and God my Father forgiving me, for long-held anger and hatred when I was 49 years old, led to freedom to *love extravagantly, give generously, live abundantly, and dance joyfully*. In other words, that forgiveness gave me the key to a new dimension of life: to walk in forgiveness and freedom. That new dimension swept change into the spiritual, emotional, familial, intellectual, and physical arenas of life. It also invaded the practical realm; it provided the freedom I needed to enter the PhD program.
11. Earning a PhD
    The path was difficult, especially at my age, but it led me to teach full time at the college and qualified me to set up a private practice, which grew into establishing Wellsprings Psychological Resources. That opened the door to found The Ark Family Preservation Center. And that toppled other dominoes:

12. Teaching Christian counseling skills at the International Center for Christian Leadership (ICCL) in Kiev, Ukraine (rotating course every 2-3 years)
13. Doing workshops on play therapy, ADHD, depression in Asian women, and many others topics in Kuala Lumpur, Malaysia during two summers
14. Co-leading weekend retreats for furloughing missionaries with Dr. Harold Rhoades for many years
15. Counseling missionaries and laypersons in England, Scotland, Germany, Italy, Romania, Ukraine, Malaysia, Japan, Hong Kong, Kenya, Uganda, Israel—and students on many airplane rides to those locations. Twelve-hour flights provide ample opportunities for heart-to-heart talks.

But, I have to admit one of the greatest effects of the lifetime of falling dominoes found flourishing expression in the establishment of Wellsprings Psychological Resources and The Ark Family Preservation Center. Those two ministries could be my greatest contributions to northeast Georgia, a legacy for future generations.

Love Him, Love Them

The power of love cannot be overestimated in the healing process of the spirit. When I first opened my private practice, I felt that I could provide therapy to the children of addicts, but not the addicts themselves. Candidly, I felt I could not accept them or their behaviors because of the damage they have done to their children. But, God would not let me hold that judgmental attitude for long.

Very soon after opening Wellsprings, I saw a steady stream of female drug addicts seeking freedom from their addictions. My heart breaks each time I hear the horror stories of how they got trapped by the lies of friends or family who led them into a life of hell. When fathers or mothers come in to tell their story, I hear the Lord speak to my heart, "Love Me by loving them." By acknowledging my own weaknesses, I can understand the weaknesses of others.

When a transgendered female appeared in my office, I thought I had no skills to help her. But God spoke to me at our first meeting, "Love her as I love her."

So, we start by loving them for Him, and we soon love them for themselves, each one a unique person, each one God's special child. Extravagant love comes only from God, but He uses human vessels to deliver it to those who need it most. I'm humbled to be one of those vessels—whether it is passing the torch to an intern or to the bruised and broken client in front of me.

Do for Them What You Would Do for Me

I often return to those two prophetic words that carved out the future development of the counseling center Wellsprings and the nonprofit ministry of The Ark. At the time of their delivery, I didn't understand it at all. Years later, when I listened to the prophecies again, I saw more clearly how God led me on this desert journey.

But that is often the way of the Lord. He brings things into existence through the spoken word. But, because His ways are not our ways, and our thoughts are not His thoughts, we may live a long time before suddenly realizing they have already come to pass.

Twenty-three years before we built Wellsprings, Ken Medema composed the prophetic song in—and about—Franklin Springs. As I described in Chapter 8, his vision for Franklin Springs imagined beautiful fountains, rising into the air, wells bubbling up from the ground. He saw the people living there as gentle, loving folks, taking you in and loving you deep. He also envisioned people coming from the north and south and east and west to behold the miracle of Franklin Springs.

And, then, two years before Wellsprings was built, Lee Grady prophesied that Paul and I had been prepared for a new assignment and would receive a new anointing. He also saw that we would face resistance, but God called us to be courageous and determined, to go against tradition, to go upstream against the flow.

I had connected *none* of these dots when I established Wellsprings and named it. When I re-listened to the Medema prophetic song two years after Wellsprings was built, I was astonished that the Wellsprings name was embedded in Medema's lyrics. God had a plan before the foundations of the earth and His plan came into fruition because we followed the Spirit's lead. I often wonder how many times I have *not* followed His voice and how many opportunities I have missed. That thought keeps me humble.

Rescuing, Restoring, and Returning

Clearly, the words of the prophets blazed the trail for Wellsprings and The Ark Family Preservation Center. I believe God spoke both into existence. And they have become platforms for our work of *rescuing, restoring, and returning.* We *rescue* God's children from tsunami flood waters of toxic environments and relationships. Then we *restore* them back to emotional, psychological, spiritual, which often impacts their physical health. Finally, when they are healthy, we *return* them to fill the role that God designed for them.

On this high point of reflecting back over my life, I can see perhaps the most important lesson Jesus gave us in His teachings: *We do for others precisely what we would do for Him.* In giving to others, our supply of love multiplies, never dwindles, and never runs dry. God withholds nothing from us; we should withhold nothing from those we are called to love.

Chapter 12

Befriending Death

I have been unusually and thankfully healthy throughout my life. So, when I was diagnosed with breast cancer in early 2019, it didn't quite compute. But I could not argue with MRI's, X-rays, and lab reports.

From the beginning I wanted to know the best and worst scenarios for my condition. On the way to Athens to see my oncologist, Paul and I talked about his mother's double mastectomy. Because I had heard horror stories of chemo treatments, I was relieved when Dr. Gunn recommended a lumpectomy followed by radiation treatment for me. His prognosis was good. His nurse commended me for having annual check-ups. The small lump was caught before it became aggressive. I felt no anxiety about the cancer diagnosis or the surgery. Had my prognosis been bleak, I may have responded differently, but still, cancer is cancer.

What blindsided me was the ordeal of daily radiation treatments following the surgery. The problem became a new iteration of John Lennon's maxim: life is what happens when we're making other plans. I had a work schedule. Clients needed me; my Wellsprings staff needed me; my family needed me. Breast cancer didn't care. It definitely threw a wrench into my work schedule. I had to come up with a plan.

Five days a week I would drive to Athens—the closest cancer center—an hour away, take a 20-minute radiation treatment, and drive an hour back to Franklin Springs. Then I would pick up my client load three hours later than I typically would, if my trip imposed no delays. In my plan I would see clients till 8:00pm, go home, do paperwork, have an hour to relax, and be in bed by 11:00 pm. Piece of cake.

When I told my family about my plan, they rejected it outright. Andeena offered to come from Oregon to Georgia to drive me to Athens daily. After all, I was 70 years old, as she pointed out. (I pointed out to her that 70 is just a 2-digit number.) Julinna suggested I come to Conway for the treatments. Wasn't there a cancer treatment center near Conway Medical Center? I started thinking...a cancer treatment center just five minutes away from our "grandchildren house" in Conway. We bought it in 2013 in order to spend more time with our grandchildren. I could be near my daughter and granddaughters. That could even add healing to my body and mind. Now, that sounded like good logic!

But questions still troubled me. Would my staff be able to manage? Of course, I would continue to handle the finances and provide supervision for interns. I realized Wellsprings would need to go on without me during my convalescence. So, big question: could Wellsprings survive as a fully functioning practice with a mature staff of therapists and office workers while I was convalescing? Could The Ark continue on without my leadership and fundraising?

At some point, I became tired of trying to figure it all out, so I let go of my illusion of control and allowed God and my capable staff to take charge. Best six weeks of my life! Not only did Wellsprings survive, they soared!

One year later, I am now in full remission with clear mammograms at each checkpoint. However, just six months after my radiation treatments ended, Paul was diagnosed with aggressive prostate cancer. We count our blessings to be able to get daily radiation treatments at a facility just a mile from our home in Conway. The initial reports following Paul's treatments suggest good results. God continues to hold us lovingly in His strong grip as we navigate through uncharted waters of ill health.

Facing Dependence

My breast cancer diagnosis did not shake me. Although I believed God could heal, I did not ask for healing. Did I believe that God could heal me? Absolutely. But, on a deeper level, I knew that God would be with me on whatever journey He led me. I didn't need to ask Him for anything. He already knew what I needed before I asked.

I've lived most of my life in the expectation that I would die young, just as my parents did. So, when I celebrated my 35th and 43rd birthdays, (my parents' ages when they died) I wondered if that would be the year of my death. When those two milestones came and went, I believed that each succeeding year was a bonus – something to celebrate beyond my expectation. Like my grandmother, perhaps, I want to die young – sometime just shy of my 100th birthday.

Instead of asking God to heal me from cancer, I asked Him to teach me what I needed to learn from my illness. I did not want to miss anything. I wanted to learn new dimensions of trust in my dance with cancer. And so, He has, and still is.

I don't fear death nearly as much as I fear dependence on others. I've taken care of myself since age 12. And, I've taken on the role of care-giver to many others in my personal and professional life. So, for me to release the helm of my ship and give it to someone else is frightening. If such a transition comes my way, I know I will need God's grace to help me face it.

But, then, I think of Jesus' life. He came into our world as a dependent baby and left it as a dependent man, hanging helplessly on a cross. He chose to give up His independence through a painful and humiliating death. If Jesus could do it, I believe He will help me handle whatever comes to me.

Befriending Death

Going through a health crisis forces us to seriously consider the end of life. During this time of my cancer diagnosis, I remembered the leukemia that took my brother Bobby's life when he was only 8 years old. I cried for years because he wasn't there to play with me. I also shed tears for many years on Mom's birthday and Mother's Day.

Looking back now, I realized that I had also grieved my dad's death, not with tears, but with intense anger. Many years later, through the process of forgiveness, I found release to grieve his death in a healthy way, which finally brought peace to my weary heart.

As a psychologist, I have studied the research on the grieving process and have helped dozens of clients express their sorrow at the death of their loved ones. I help them to see that tears are a gift and grief is the price we pay for loving others.

As I thought of the possibility of my own death, I realized that we humans tend to ignore death by staying busy. That's no way to live, and it's no way to die. Through the writings of Henri Nouwen, I began to see that death may be the greatest gift we receive from God. And it can be the greatest gift we leave to those we love. Because God's love never dies, love is greater than death. It is simply a passageway into our new home.

When we befriend our own death, we can become truly caring people. As Nouwen observes, "befriending our death allows us to see the face of Jesus in the poor, the addicted, those who live with AIDS and cancer, the transgendered."[16]

I want to live well, and I want to die well. I want to befriend my death so it can become my best gift to the people of my world—those I bore, those I held, those I cared for, those I love so much. We are brothers and sisters. We are all born as fragile beings; we all die as fragile beings. We need each other to live well and to die well.

When Jesus rose from the dead, He spoke the words that bring comfort when we face death, "Be not afraid." Those three simple words contain all you or I need to live life freely, victoriously, and unencumbered by the cares of life or the fear of death. His words are true and the basis for hope; they evict the demons that seem to come in the night.

If we truly believe that indeed Jesus died that most horrible death on the cross and that He rose from the dead, ... *if we truly believe* that He overcame death and has promised the same for us... *if we truly believe* that death is the gateway to resurrection life with Him ... then why do we fear death? Do we fear the pain? Or do we fear the unknown or uncontrollable? But, the fact is, we do have fears. We are human, and God understands that we go to dark places when we are afraid.

But, Jesus doesn't ask us to overcome our fears alone or out of our own reservoirs. He says in Matthew 28:20: "And surely I am with you always, to the very end of the age." Even through this dreadful pandemic of Covid-19, even through cancer and Alzheimer's disease, He is with us always. We are secure.

16 Henri Nouwen, *Our Greatest Gift: A Meditation on Dying and* Caring (New York: HarperCollins Publishers, 1994)

Unfinished Work

I wonder if Moses felt like a failure at the end of his life. While he led his fellow Hebrews from slavery, his real purpose was to lead them to the Promised Land. But he didn't quite make it. He was able to see it from the top of Mt. Nebo, but he wasn't allowed to go in. But, come to think of it, Moses *did* enter the Promised Land when he appeared with Jesus and Elijah on the Mount of Transfiguration after Jesus' death and resurrection (Mark 9:2-5). And entering the Land of Promise with Jesus had to be better than with the Israelites!

I often wonder if I will feel like a failure at the end of my life. When I look around, I see so much more I could have done. So much unfinished business. Do any of us ever finish our work? After all, it is *His* work. I believe He looks at the whole line of servants, each of whom completes a small portion of His work.

The Bible tells stories of people who served God's purpose in their generation. Then, after listing many heroes who endured great hardships, Hebrews tells us: "...none of them received what had been promised, since God had planned something better for us so that only together with us would they be made perfect." (Hebrews 11:39-40)

I most certainly haven't done it perfectly, but I have tried to serve God's purpose for my time. God gave me the dream of The Ark Family Preservation Center. But the fulfillment of that dream lies far beyond my abilities. I cannot make it happen. Trust me, I have tried. Knowing I cannot do it on my own gives me the assurance that God has a plan for completion of The Ark. When it's time for me to complete my part, I believe God will direct me to pass the torch to the one behind me. As that Hebrews passage suggests, if God had planned something better, He will see the work completed in partnership with others. For me, for all of us who join in that great line of workers, we must, like athletes, leave it all on the field. Hold nothing back. If we still have resources in reserve, we haven't done all we could.

In the final scene of Steven Spielberg's *Schindler's List,* German industrialist Oskar Schindler stood surrounded by 1,200 Jews, thanking him for saving their lives during the Holocaust. But, in that moment, Schindler realized if he had sold his car, his lapel pin, or gold ring, he could have saved even more lives. He wept bitterly as he fully grasped the reality of how he selfishly held insignificant possessions in reserve instead of selling them to save more lives.

I wonder if I will be held accountable for holding back trivial trinkets or wasting my time when people's lives could have been saved. I know I can't save the world, but I might be able to save one more. And that one more is precious to God.

My Legacy

Writing a memoir takes authors, including me, back over the past. But now I want to look forward. Because of my Soul Companion's great love for me and His gift of salvation, I want to leave a legacy for those coming behind me. Leaving a legacy for the next generation means different things for different people. Some want their name inscribed on a monument, a building named after them, a law that carries their name, or a legacy of official athletic, academic, business, or other records of achievement. Any of them could be worthwhile legacies, but that's not the kind I want to leave.

Today, as I was writing this part of the chapter, the mother of one of my previous psychology students at Emmanuel College contacted me. A month ago, her son completed his doctorate of education in counseling. She looked me up to thank me for encouraging him to stay in college some 12 years ago when he was discouraged and thinking of dropping out. She told me, "He mentions Dr. Oxley's impact on him often." She just wanted me to know. That kind of phone call keeps me in the trenches, renewing my spirit to keep working for as long as He energizes me. That's the legacy I care about – the one written on human hearts.

My greatest legacy to those who come after me may be wrapped in this vital message from God: "You are my beloved child – no matter what you've done or haven't done. I love you and will always love you. Life is messy and unpredictable. But, with Me in your life, we can weather the storms and enjoy a life-giving relationship. I have a path designed uniquely for you. I'm extending my hand of friendship to you. Let's do this journey together." This kind of unconditional love that Christ offers us overcomes our inner demons of rejection, abandonment, feeling useless and unwanted, desiring invisibility, and perhaps the worst fear of all: feeling no real purpose in life.

Moses's life story ends with a simple statement that "God buried him in Moab ... Since then, no prophet has risen in Israel like Moses, whom the Lord knew face to face." (Deuteronomy 34:6, 10) Moses and God obviously had a rare, beautiful relationship. The Bible reveals surprising heart-to-heart conversations. More surprising, God had so much affection for Moses that He arranged a private burial with only Himself attending. Now that's a noteworthy legacy!

I've learned much about how to relate to God through the study of many Biblical characters. With the exception of Jesus, Moses's life has impacted me more than any other. He had many flaws, but God chose him. Not in spite of those failings, but because of them. God chose Moses not because of his bravery, wisdom, or leadership, but because of his humility. God knew he could trust Moses to carry out His work. The Bible does describe Moses as "a very humble man, more humble than anyone else on the face of the earth" (Numbers 12:3).

Moses knew he couldn't fulfill God's plan without others. He needed judges, spies, warriors, singers, and priests. He also depended on Aaron as his translator and spokesperson. In the end, Moses couldn't even take the children of Israel into the Promised Land of Canaan. He needed one he trained, Joshua, to finish the work.

None of us can do it alone. Our culture insists we can, but real life begs to differ. The voices of our times proclaim independence. But God created us for relationship. Whether we like it or not, we are all dependent on others. And God always sends the help we need.

Jesus captured the beauty of relationship when He called His disciples "friends." And the Bible names Abraham and Moses as friends of God. According to James 2:23, "'Abraham *believed God*, and it was credited to him as righteousness,' and he was called God's friend." Even before meeting my Soul Companion as a 9-year-old, *I believed God*. Somehow, I stood away from the deceptions I encountered as a child and chose to believe God. And He has stood with me as my Friend through the years.

As I look back over the journey, I thank Him for the invitation to live out a full and delightful friendship with Him. We've walked together through national crises, too many cemeteries, wrecks on Route 66, needles in the ER, failures and forgiveness, mysteries and mercies, and many miles through love and marriage and motherhood and grandchildren. We—my Friend and I—built an Ark and a counseling center, tackled jobs that were not even close to "age-appropriate," and embraced desert storms and desert dances together. Always, *together*.

Now, in the words of Robert Frost: "I have promises to keep, And miles to go before I sleep."[17] I look forward to the rest of the journey toward my promised land.

17 Robert Frost, "Stopping by Woods on a Snowy Evening" from *The Poetry of Robert Frost*, edited by Edward Connery Lathem. Copyright 1923, © 1969 by Henry Holt and Company, Inc., renewed 1951, by Robert Frost. Reprinted with the permission of Henry Holt and Company, LLC.

Appreciation

I concur with David's words in Psalm 16: 5-6, "LORD, you alone are my portion and my cup; you make my lot secure. The boundary lines have fallen for me in pleasant places; surely I have a delightful inheritance."

I'm grateful for and to many who fill up my inheritance:

That great cloud of witnesses on the other side: generations of the departed who served God faithfully, leaving a blueprint for me to follow.

Moses, who is a pattern for living, as much for his failures as his successes. I will always appreciate and learn from his fortitude and authenticity.

My spiritual guides who illuminated vital points along my circuitous journey. I appreciate their encouragement to stay on the path, even if I see only the next step in front of me.

Mother Teresa for the wisdom imparted through her books and life of service to others.

A.D. Beacham, Jr. for his pastoral care and insights into scripture which nourishes his flock.

Lee Grady for his prophetic sensitivity.

Ken Medema for inspiring me with a vision for Franklin Springs as a place of healing.

Bill Kuert for challenging me to start writing this memoir.

Martha at the Monastery of the Holy Spirit for her ardent spiritual insight.

Angel Davis for inviting Jesus to speak to me in our counseling sessions.

My grandparents, Fletcher and Gladys Clinkenbeard, John and Gertrude Harris, and my parents Christopher Columbus Harris and Flora Belle Clinkenbeard for giving me a fine mixture of genes and personality traits.

My Wellsprings family, close friends, and clients who enrich my life with love, laughter, and light.

My trainees, interns, and young friends who have grabbed the torch and run with it.

Our Dinners 8 group (John & Judy, Cindy & Mike, Harold & Candy) who have been friends for more than 23 years. I thank them for their presence in times of crisis and celebration.

Aunt Lorene and Uncle Leon Crosswhite, who pulled me and my siblings from the swirling waters of uncertainty and fear after our parents' deaths. I thank them for bringing us into a safe harbor.

My nieces and nephews, aunts, uncles, and in-laws who have inspired me with honesty, integrity, and laughter.

My cousins who spark joy when we gather, and for their generous contributions to the Clinkenbeard Gardens.

Ken, Carol, and Chris, my siblings, who have traveled this journey alongside me even though we live in four states and meet infrequently; they have given generously to make my dream of The Ark a reality. Our respect for each other grows with each passing mile.

My granddaughters, Marigny and Parisa, who are the winds filling my sails and the laughter in my spirit. We sail farther and more joyfully than I could possibly sail alone.

My daughters, Julinna and Andeena, whose passions have enlarged my world. Our different perspectives on issues only deepen my admiration for them.

Paul, my husband who has been faithful to me and has faith in me. I would not be the person I am today without his willingness to support God's call on my life.

My Soul Companion who befriended me at age nine and has guided me throughout my astounding journey of life.

The splendid reviewers of this manuscript— Doug Beacham, John Boaz, Jan Brown, Sally Knox, Shanna Kohr, Bill Kuert, Chris Maxwell, Amy McArthy, and Summer Sneed.

My editor, Ed Chinn, who encouraged me onward, challenged me, and took out huge chunks of my writing "for the sake of the reader." Without his keen eye for keeping the story moving, this memoir would have been bogged in mire and gone awry. His patience knows no end!